Dec 2002

Rumrunners & Revenuers:
Prohibition in Vermont

Bob,

Best wishes

[signature]

Rumrunners & Revenuers: Prohibition in Vermont

by
Scott Wheeler

Edited by
Christopher A. Bray

The New England Press, Inc.
Shelburne, Vermont

© 2002 by Scott Wheeler

First Edition
Book Design and Production by Christopher A. Bray

Library of Congress Catalog Card Number: 2002115779
ISBN 1-881535-44-4
Printed in the United States of America
06 05 04 03 02   5 4 3 2

This book set in Cheltenham 10.5/13.5
Titling in ITC Kabel

For additional copies or a catalog of our other titles, please write:
The New England Press
P.O. Box 575
Shelburne, Vermont 05482
or e-mail: *nep@together.net*

Visit us on the Web at *www.nepress.com*

To my wife, Penny,
and children, Curtis, Nicholas, and Emily

"The best way to kill something in Vermont
is to mandate it."
Governor Richard Snelling

"Freedom and Unity"
Vermont State Motto

Contents

Preface

From 1920 to 1933 rumrunners roamed, and in some cases, even ruled, everything from America's city streets to the rural, dirt roads of Vermont. Those days are long gone. Vermont accounts of the era survive in aging memories and in the yellowing, crumbling pages of the period's newspapers, some of which have long since ceased publication. Although much has been written about Prohibition's effects on America, little has been recorded about its impact on Vermont and Vermonters. This book, particularly with its oral histories given by first-hand participants in Prohibition, is a start toward preserving the stories of that era.

I heard my first Prohibition stories long before I ever dreamed of this book. Thirty years ago, as I grew up in Newport, Vermont—a community several miles from the Quebec border and deep in the heart of Vermont's Northeast Kingdom—I listened to family, friends, and visitors tell tales of Prohibition-era events.

I learned that my town and all of northern Vermont had been on the front lines of Prohibition. Vermont, divided from wet Canada by a relatively unguarded border, sparsely populated and connected by thousands of miles of winding dirt roads with very few lawmen on them, had been ideal for smugglers.

I heard rumors of famous gun-toting gangsters passing through Vermont's northern border communities on their way to Quebec to arrange for huge shipments of alcohol. I also heard stories of homegrown outlaws. Many of their faces were those of ordinary Vermonters, not those of big-time criminals; some were the faces of desperation—a desperation driven by the curse of alcoholism or, more commonly, by the need to feed a hungry family. During the second half of Prohibition, Vermont's economy, especially in the border communities, was struggling. It sank further when the Stock Market Crash of 1929 sent the U.S. into the Great Depression.

Many of the Vermonters who broke Prohibition laws went on to lead productive lives as law-abiding citizens. For some families the brief stint on the wrong side of the law is considered a badge of honor. Some smugglers became folk heroes, and their Prohibition escapades have grown more flamboyant and daring as the years have passed. For other families the walk on the wrong side of the law is a badge of shame, not to be spoken about, but buried, hoping people will forget.

Most of the people who lived through Prohibition are now gone. This book attempts to capture a cross section of the personal remembrances of the few Vermonters who have clear memories of the period. I interviewed bootleggers and moonshiners as well as teetotalers and the children of lawmen. I spoke with others who were simply caught in the middle; they represent the ordinary country folk who watched Vermont's roads turned into raceways punctuated by gunshots piercing the night air. Whether one was for, against, or indifferent to the law, it affected every Vermonter.

Alcohol is a billion dollar industry in America today. Readers may find it hard to imagine that beer, wine and spirits were ever banned, but Prohibition was not without ample precedent. Numerous temperance movements predate Prohibition by up to one hundred years.

The book's two introductory chapters elucidate the historical context that produced Prohibition. Readers will learn, for example, that Vermont was dry for all but one year between 1847 and 1903, when state control was ceded to the municipalities. This statutory legacy lives on, and five Vermont towns remain dry even today.

The next fourteen chapters are the heart of the book: the interviews with those who lived through Prohibition.

The book concludes with "The Border Today," in which readers will learn that smuggling is timeless—it predated Prohibition by centuries and it continues today.

Acknowledgments

It's impossible for me to thank everybody who helped in my research. Here are some of the people whose contributions were particularly important.

Deadlines, frustrations, computer crashes, unending trips around the state, and more—my wife, Penny, and children, Curtis, Nicholas, and Emily, have seen it all in the last three years. I thank them for their support and patience.

My parents, Wayne and Pauline Wheeler, raised me in an atmosphere of history. My father collected antiques, or, as I called them at the time, "junk." His love of history and anything old rubbed off on me.

My former co-workers at the *Chronicle* in Barton, Vermont helped inspire me to write this book. Special thanks to the paper's owner, Chris Braithwaite, who is the ultimate boss and a kind and compassionate human being. Tena Starr, a former editor at the newspaper, played a key role in making this book become reality. She taught me more than how to be a good reporter; she instilled in me the importance of writing an objective story without abandoning the truth or resorting to sensationalism.

Author Howard Frank Mosher offered good advice and played a key role. Not only did he believe in the importance of this book, but he also instilled confidence in me and directed me to the New England Press.

Vermont state archivist Gregory Sanford is probably one of the most brilliant and helpful people that I have ever met. He was instrumental in my research.

I received generous help in locating period photographs from a number of individuals: Don Miner of the St. Albans Historical Society; Joan Cowans of the Canaan Historical Society, who provided photographs from the organization's archives as well as her own; Roger Miller; Joyce Weldon; Citizens Utilities, Derby; and Paul

Carnahan, librarian at the Vermont Historical Society in Barre, who located both photographs and documents. People who provided picture postcards and other memorabilia include Benny and Karol Curtis of Brownington, Vermont; Reg Alexander of Brownington; and Dale Woods of Newport, Vermont.

Pastors Dr. Fred Barker and Carol Ann Barker of Derby, Vermont blessed me with continued friendship and spiritual guidance throughout the three years it took me to compile and write this book.

I would also like to thank two members of the United States Border Patrol. Ed Duda was the Assistant Chief of the Vermont and northeastern New York patrol sectors at the time that he assisted me; he is now stationed in Buffalo, New York as a Deputy Chief. John Pfeifer is currently Patrol Agent in Charge at the Newport, Vermont station; John provided invaluable help in finding photographs and documentation of the Border Patrol's early history.

Steve Pike, U.S. Customs Inspector at the Highgate border crossing, was instrumental in helping me locate key documents and individuals.

Thanks to the New England Press. Managing Editor Christopher Bray helped develop the manuscript and crafted the finished book. Editor Mark Wanner aided me in the book's earliest stages. Working with them was a pleasure.

I saved the most important and generous people for last—the people I interviewed. Whereas some people would prefer to forget Prohibition, these folks, the surviving few of their generation, realized the importance of sharing and preserving their stories and recollections. Their stories are part of Vermont's story.

Last, I imagine that this book will draw out more anecdotes and memories of the period. I hope that readers interested in contributing to my ongoing explorations into Prohibition and Vermont history will contact me. This book marks not an end to my work, but more of a milestone along the way. Readers can reach me at *The Kingdom Historical*, a periodical and website, found on the internet at *www.thekingdomhistorical.com*.

—Derby, Vermont
November, 2002

Rumrunners & Revenuers: Prohibition in Vermont

A Brief History of Prohibition in America

"Eighteenth Amendment Is Dead:
President Roosevelt Proclaims
the Repeal of Prohibition"

Nearly every paper in the country led with this headline or one comparable on December 6, 1933. Prohibition had been repealed, and for the first time in thirteen years, alcohol was legal. The Great Experiment was over. Prohibition had polarized the nation, cost the country millions of dollars and many lives, and in the eyes of many, did more harm than good.

The Roots of National Prohibition

In nineteenth-century America, alcohol never achieved the level of cultural acceptance that it had in Europe. Here, alcohol was extolled for its relaxing, convivial effects, and even for its mind-altering properties; yet it was also blamed for a wide variety of medical and societal problems. Over the years alcohol has been cited as a contributing factor of insanity, epilepsy, family dysfunction, divorce, poverty, child desertion, and crime.

Though federal Prohibition began in 1920, efforts to prohibit or at least limit alcohol consumption began more than a century earlier. The Total Abstinence Society was formed in Portland, Maine, in 1815. By 1840, Portland became the nation's first "dry" city. Under the leadership of Neal Dow, "The Father of Prohibition," the Maine legislature approved a total ban on the manufacture and sale of liquor in 1851. This law, though modified over time, remained in effect until Prohibition ended in 1933.

The movement to ban alcohol was widespread and emerged in various places and times. Two particularly influential movements were the Women's Christian Temperance Union (WCTU), still in operation today, and the Anti-Saloon League. The WCTU grew out of the Women's Temperance Crusades of 1873–1874 in New York and Ohio, where groups of women knelt in prayer in saloons—or outside them when denied entry—to pressure the establishments to stop serving alcohol. The movement was amazingly effective, and in a mere fifty days eradicated liquor sales in over two hundred and fifty Ohio towns and villages.

The WCTU, founded by Eliza Thompson in 1874, and subsequently headed by Frances Willard, was not a single-issue organization. While their best-known efforts were directed at eliminating alcohol, tobacco, and drug use, they saw this mission in the context of an overarching concern: "protection of the home." Empowered by Willard's energy—her motto was "Do everything"—the WCTU grew by 1896 to thirty-nine departments, twenty-five of which targeted non-temperance programs such as the protection of women and children at home and at work, the eight-hour workday, the right of labor to organize, the establishment of kindergartens, and women's suffrage. That the country was in need of such reforms can be gleaned from financial statistics: In 1900, Americans were spending over one billion dollars a year on alcohol, versus nine hundred million a year on meat, and only two hundred million a year on public education.

In the Midwest, and in neighboring states such as Kansas, alcohol was also a contentious issue. During the early frontier days, one of the first businesses to open in many towns was a saloon. Often these establishments brought with them drinking, smoking, gambling, and prostitution. Profitable, popular, and often powerful, saloons thrived, and lawlessness was all too commonly a fact of life in many communities. As the "Wild West" moved further west, however, communities were becoming more civilized, and less lenient toward the mayhem associated with many saloons.

One of the main reasons early saloons had been tolerated was financial: They brought much-needed business and income to towns, and they even generated significant municipal income in the form of fines. As the towns and their economies matured in the second half of the nineteenth century, saloons came under increasing pressure to clean up their acts. Kansas, for instance, passed an amendment to the state's constitution in 1881 that outlawed alcohol for all but industrial, scientific, and medicinal uses.

One of the most colorful and best-known anti-alcohol agitators was WCTU member Carry Nation. Living in a supposedly alcohol-free Kansas, Nation saw many alcohol-related problems in her community, most poignantly the suffering of women and children when fathers drank away money needed for proper food, clothing, and shelter. Frustrated by poorly enforced prohibition laws, Nation began her own anti-alcohol campaign, calling her fellow members "Home Supporters." From 1899 through 1901, Nation—armed with a Bible in one hand and her trademark hatchet in the other—began to lead raids on illegal saloons in Kansas.

Arrested many times, and bailed out just as regularly, Nation sparked the prohibition cause. After two years' rampage, Nation foreswore any further hatchet raids on saloons, and thereafter she traveled throughout the United States and overseas speaking out about temperance as well as other reforms, including women's suffrage, women's health, and smoking. For the next ten years, until her death in 1911, Nation spoke to crowds in carnival tents, on vaudeville stages, and even in Carnegie Hall, broadening and strengthening the growing prohibitionist sentiment in America.

Less colorful than Nation, but ultimately more effective, was The Anti-Saloon League. Founded in Ohio in 1893, the League focused its efforts exclusively on eliminating alcohol from the bars and "joints" of the time. Its em-

This poster was used to promote one of Nation's many speaking tours, which brought her before audiences in America, Canada, and overseas.

phatic motto was unequivocal: "The saloon must go." The group pledged its support to any politician, Republican or Democrat, who favored the abolition of alcohol. Funded by various church groups, through which the League also spread its message, the group campaigned precinct by precinct to make towns, cities, counties, and, eventually, whole states dry. In 1913, after twenty years of success at the local level, the League shifted its focus to Washington, where it pushed for national prohibition.

Wayne Wheeler, head lobbyist for the League, and also known as the "dry boss," spearheaded efforts in Washington. Though the League-sponsored Hobson-Shepard bill was defeated in Congress in 1914, national prohibition was suddenly a very real possibility.

While the actions of the Women's Christian Temperance Union, Carry Nation, and the Anti-Saloon League all worked to make prohibition a near reality, it was World War I that finally provided the impetus for Congress to pass prohibition legislation. Once the United States had entered the war on April 6, 1917, prohibitionists began to use the war to their advantage. Members of the Saloon

"Daddy's in there. Our shoes, and stockings and clothes and food are in there, too, and they'll never come out."
This cartoon appeared in a 1927 issue of the *Chicago Sun Times.*

League and other temperance groups noted the irony of American men going off to battle the Germans in Europe while back at home, brewers and distillers of German ancestry were reaping huge profits as they led Americans toward moral decay.

Wheeler and the League rallied around a new slogan: "Kaiserism abroad and booze at home must go."

Anti-alcohol lobbyists, as well as a growing number of politicians, argued that a country at war should not waste grain by turning it into alcohol—it should be saved for the troops. Those who argued against prohibition were increasingly branded as unpatriotic.

The Prohibition movement was also supported by one of the largest political groups of the time—the Ku Klux Klan. Although now best known for their racist views, many Klan members professed Christian values, which included temperance. Although shunned today, the Klan held tremendous power during the early years of the twentieth century. This power was thrown behind the forces arguing for national prohibition legislation.

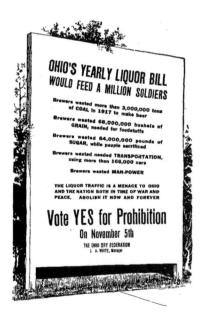

This poster from the Ohio Dry Federation decried the use of grains and other resources for brewing rather than feeding our boys fighting "over there," in Europe.

The Anti-Saloon League and other temperance organizations created a great deal of literature and many posters to dramatize their campaign. Shown above is a poster used in a statewide referendum to make Ohio a dry state. The League and its allies deftly and successfully equated patriotic support for the military with support for prohibition.

The Eighteenth Amendment

Feeling the mounting pressure generated by the Saloon League and its allies, an increasing number of politicians agreed to support prohibition. On December 18, 1917, the Sixty-fifth Congress of the United States proposed the Eighteenth Amendment to the Constitution, outlawing the manufacture, sale, or transportation of intoxicating liquors in the U.S.:

> Section 1. After one year from the ratification of this article the manufacture, sale, or transportation of intoxicating liquors within, the importation thereof into, or the exportation thereof from the United States and all territory subject to the jurisdiction thereof for beverage purposes is hereby prohibited.

> Section 2. The Congress and the several states shall have concurrent power to enforce this article by appropriate legislation.

> Section 3. This article shall be inoperative unless it shall have been ratified as an amendment to the Constitution by the legislatures of the several states, as provided in the Constitution, within seven years from the date of the submission hereof to the states by the Congress.

For the amendment to become law it had to be ratified by thirty-six of the then forty-eight states within a period of seven years. The anti-prohibition forces gravely miscalculated when they assumed that this seven-year window provided ample time to fight the amendment's ratification. Three weeks later, on January 8, 1918, Mississippi became the first state to vote for ratification. Only a year later, on January 16, 1919—when a final flurry of ratifications passed in Nebraska, North Carolina, Utah, Missouri, and Wyoming—the amendment became the law of the land.

It wasn't until after national ratification that several other states voted for ratification, including Vermont. The rapid passage of the amendment surprised even those who fought for Prohibition. Reveling in their triumph, some prohibitionists insisted that the temperance movement advance to a worldwide stage in a push for universal prohibition.

Prohibition officially took effect at 12:01 A.M., January 17, 1920. The law gave the country one year to prepare to become "dry." Though intended to be a time for people to consume or eliminate

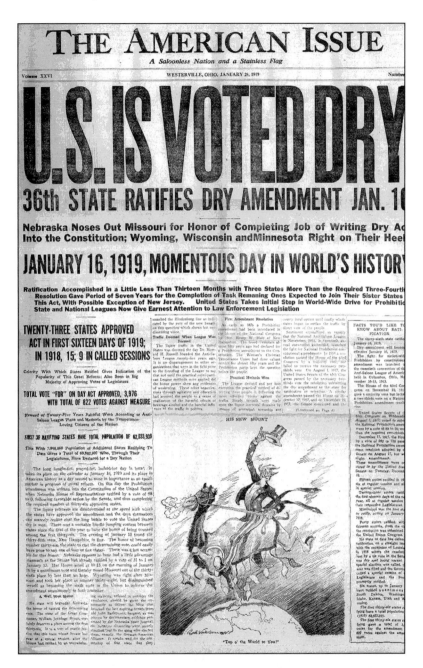

THE AMERICAN ISSUE

A Saloonless Nation and a Stainless Flag

Volume XXVI   WESTERVILLE, OHIO, JANUARY 25, 1919   Number

U.S. IS VOTED DRY

36th STATE RATIFIES DRY AMENDMENT JAN. 1

Nebraska Noses Out Missouri for Honor of Completing Job of Writing Dry Ac Into the Constitution; Wyoming, Wisconsin and Minnesota Right on Their Heel

JANUARY 16, 1919, MOMENTOUS DAY IN WORLD'S HISTOR

Ratification Accomplished in a Little Less Than Thirteen Months with Three States More Than the Required Three-Fourth Resolution Gave Period of Seven Years for the Completion of Task Remaning Ones Expected to Join Their Sister States This Act, With Possible Exception of New Jersey.   **United States Takes Initial Step in World-Wide Drive for Prohibitio State and National Leagues Now Give Earnest Attention to Law Enforcement Legislation**

TWENTY-THREE STATES APPROVED ACT IN FIRST SIXTEEN DAYS OF 1919; IN 1918, 15; 9 IN CALLED SESSIONS

Celerity With Which States Ratified Gives Indication of the Popularity of This Great Reform; Also Seen in Big Majority of Approving Votes of Legislators

TOTAL VOTE "FOR" ON DAY ACT APPROVED, 3,976 WITH TOTAL OF 822 VOTES AGAINST MEASURE

Reward of Twenty-Five Years Faithful Work According to Anti-Saloon League Plans and Methods by the Temperance-Loving Citizens of the Nation

FIRST 36 RATIFYING STATES HAVE TOTAL POPULATION OF 62,033,939

"Top o' the World to You!"

FACTS YOU'D LIKE TO KNOW ABOUT RATIFICATION

HIS NEW MOUNT

An ebullient and sober Uncle Sam celebrates the ratification of Prohibition as he rides "His New Mount," a camel—an animal noted for its ability to thrive in "dry" climates. As Uncle Sam crosses America, he calls out "Top of the World to You!" in this cartoon featured on page one of the *American Issue*, the official paper of the Anti-Saloon League.

their supplies of alcohol, the year instead became for many Americans a time of secretive hoarding, as people stashed away beer, wine, and liquor.

The amendment didn't provide answers for several crucial questions. For example, what was to be considered an intoxicating beverage? How was the ban to be enforced, and by whom? And what were the penalties for violating the provisions of the amendment? The Volstead Act, which survived the veto of President Woodrow Wilson and was passed on October 27, 1919, provided the answers.

The Act, named after Minnesota Congressman Andrew Volstead, outlined all the rules and regulations of enforcement. It defined an intoxicating beverage as any beverage with at least a 0.5-percent alcohol content. Enforcement powers were put into the hands of the Internal Revenue Service, under the guidance of the Treasury Department. IRS officials were given the power to seize and sell cars, trucks, boats, and any other type of vehicle used to transport alcohol in violation of the Volstead Act.

The IRS also created the Prohibition Bureau, which hired approximately fifteen hundred agents, popularly known as "revenuers," to enforce the law. Although few in number, those involved in the alcohol trade feared them because, unlike many local and state officers, these federal men were renowned for their hardnosed, incorruptible professionalism. First-time violators of the Volstead Act were subject to fines of up to $1,000 and a jail term of six months. People convicted of a subsequent violation faced a possible fine of $10,000 and a five-year prison sentence. Ironically, neither the amendment nor the Volstead Act prohibited the purchase or consumption of alcohol, creating a loophole that weakened both the implementation and enforcement of the Prohibition laws.

The "Business"

Soon after Prohibition became law, legislators and lawmen began to learn that while the concept of Prohibition might have looked good on paper, the enforcement of it was all but impossible. Lawmen were hopelessly outnumbered and were unable to prevent alcohol from flooding over the borders from Canada and Mexico. Along the coasts, ships, often from nearby island nations like Bermuda and the Bahamas, would arrive under the cover of night to offload liquor to smaller ships, which either ran it ashore or stayed at sea for the evening, acting as floating saloons.

While many in Congress had been willing to vote in favor of Prohibition, they were far less willing to allocate the funds necessary for meaningful enforcement. The law became an underfunded mandate, and state and local lawmen were asked to fill in the gap. All too often, however, local agencies were already burdened with their own enforcement work. Without the financial support to hire needed help, departments across the country struggled unhappily to implement the statutes.

There was ample opportunity for enforcement. In New York City, for instance, after only two years of Prohibition, there were already an estimated five thousand illegal bars—speakeasies. After calling for federal assistance and receiving little help, New York decided in 1924 to limit its enforcement efforts. By 1927, the number of speakeasies in the city had ballooned to thirty thousand.

There was a lot of money to be made in the illegal alcohol trade, commonly referred to as "the business." In 1924, the U.S. Department of Commerce estimated the value of illegal liquor in the U.S. at about forty

A would-be speakeasy patron knocks at the locked door. The small peep hole permits those inside to verify the identity of the visitor before allowing him or her inside to join the private and illegal party.

million dollars. Huge amounts of alcohol flowed across the international borders in cars, wagons, trains, and boats, destined for urban and rural communities across America. Canada, for instance, became a major supplier to the United States, as evidenced by its startling increase in annual per capita alcohol sales. Before Prohibition, the average Canadian was purchasing 9 gallons of alcohol per year; during Prohibition this figure jumped to 102 gallons. Assuming that Canadians didn't actually change their drinking habits, this leaves each Canadian citizen with an "extra" 93 gallons—most of which very likely found its way illegally into the United States.

Following the laws of supply and demand, alcohol prices varied regionally. In border regions alcohol was not expensive, due to the relative ease of importing it, but in America's heartland, prices soared, and "the business" was very profitable. The wealthy could afford to drink, but the poor had just two options: stay dry or make their own booze. Illegal stills flourished in America, tucked away in attics, cellars, barns, and caves, far from the prying eyes of revenuers and other lawmen.

The couriers of the ever-growing alcohol trade were known as smugglers, bootleggers, and rumrunners. Their illegal jobs were dangerous, sometimes deadly, but the high pay apparently made it worth the risks. Gangs grew and prospered on the business of satisfying America's thirst for alcohol. The notorious Chicago gangster, Al Capone, created a financial empire that rivaled many corporations of the time. Controlling much of Chicago by means of his army of seven hundred gangsters, Capone's income in 1929 was estimated at 105 million dollars: 60 in illegal alcohol, 25 in illegal gambling establishments, and 20 from vice and racketeering. In current money, this makes his annual income approximately 1 billion dollars.

Though many Prohibition violators were arrested, the lucrative pay meant that replacements were easily found. Between 1920 and 1930, agents made more than 500,000 arrests for alcohol violations; 696,933 stills were seized between 1921 and 1925 alone. Yet millions of gallons of beer and liquor flowed into the country. Estimates suggest that Prohibition Bureau agents managed to stop a mere 5 percent of the smugglers and put only 10 percent of the stills out of business.

With the increased value of "the business" and the increased number of arrests, came increased violence. Capone's Chicago gang was estimated to have murdered over five hundred members of rival gangs. An examination of the U.S. Department of Commerce's "Murder Statistics from Statistical Abstract of the United States" reveals that during Prohibition, the murder rate increased nearly 40 percent, and in the decade following repeal, the rate dropped back to its pre-Prohibition levels.

The job of enforcing the Volstead Act was dangerous. Although many people in the illegal alcohol trade had no intention of shooting anybody, especially a lawman, there were some that wouldn't think twice about killing anyone in their way. Many local, county, state, and federal lawmen died in the line of duty. Amongst federal agents alone, there were sixty-five deaths between 1920 and 1929.

Even in seemingly quiet Vermont, lawmen died and were seriously injured in the line of duty. U.S. Customs Agent Anson Clark, based in Newport, Vermont, was in many scrapes, including this one described by his daughter, Frances Flanders, of Springfield, Vermont:

> "In 1923 my father and another officer unsuccessfully tried to stop a bootlegger. They chased a car down Route 5 to Lyndonville, and at some point my father managed to get on the running board of the car and was trying to persuade the driver to stop. The bootleggers, though, had no intention of stopping, and they went around a corner fast, trying to throw my father off. He was still hanging on when somebody whacked him on the side of the head with what we figured was probably the butt of a pistol. The blow knocked him off the speeding car, and he was laid up all summer. His eyesight was never correct after that; he always had to wear glasses."

Vermont lawmen died from shootings and accidents, and even drowned while battling bootleggers on Lake Champlain.

Bootleggers also lost their lives in this ongoing battle. There are many written accounts of lawmen using their guns to stop fleeing cars. While one officer drove, another officer would hang out the window and shoot. The more brazen officers stood on the car's running boards to fire. They would take aim for the fleeing car's tires or the gas tank, which was typically mounted in the rear of

This vehicle shows four bullet holes in the back, including three in the gas tank. The shots, fired by pursuing policemen, were sufficient to make this bootlegger surrender.

the car. More often than not the technique worked, and the chase ended relatively peacefully. Other times, though, an officer mistakenly ended up putting a bullet in the back of the renegade driver's head, bringing the chase to a fatal end.

As the "Roaring Twenties" ended, it was clear that the country had adopted a law it either could not or would not enforce. The federal government never created a sufficiently large corps of agents to combat alcohol, and it never made the pay attractive enough to help protect its agents from the lure of bribery. At the outset of Prohibition, when the U.S. population was 106 million, there were only 1,520 federal agents. By 1930, the U.S. population had grown by 17 million; the number of agents had only grown by 1,316. The agents' 1930 salaries were modest, between $2,300 and $2,800 annually. In contrast, the bootleggers paid seductively well: One St. Albans, Vermont, Customs agent was offered $15,000 per month to let train carloads of liquor pass through his inspection station. Not surprisingly, many lawmen supplemented their incomes by participating in the lucrative world of illegal alcohol. As lawmen increasingly became involved in the business, the public's respect for the law diminished and its support waned.

The Beginning of the End

Just as World War I, a force outside of the pro and con prohibition camps, helped bring in Prohibition, it was once again a great event that helped usher it out. The stock market crash of October 29, 1929, derailed the economy of the entire country. Within six months of the crash, four million Americans were out of work. The country slid into the Great Depression, and anti-temperance forces seized the opportunity to derail Prohibition as well. They argued that if alcohol were legalized, some two million jobs would be created, and the government would again take in substantial tax revenues. Their case seemed ever more compelling as the depression continued to deepen and work became more difficult to find. By early 1931, the number of unemployed had jumped to eight million. By year's end, it had soared to thirteen million. It would only get worse.

The 1932 unemployment statistics for this country were staggering: Nearly 50 percent of the workforce couldn't find jobs. Even those who managed to hold on to their jobs saw their wages drop by half or more. Families seeking government aid received only $2.39 a week. The country was thrown into turmoil. Millions of

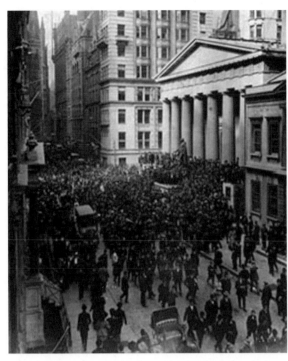

The stock market crash of October 1929 did what no anti-Prohibitionist could achieve: It helped unravel support for the Eighteenth Amendment and the Volstead Act. In the years that followed the crash, the economics of legalizing alcohol began to outweigh the ethical and social considerations underpinning Prohibition.

people were in desperate straits—some literally starving to death—and there was little anybody could do to help them.

The Depression made Prohibition, already unpopular, an anathema in many circles. With so many people suffering and lacking basic needs, the battle against alcohol seemed a misplaced effort. The lure of fast and easy money from working in the business became more and more difficult to resist. Honorable, law-abiding citizens joined the ranks of rumrunners and speakeasy proprietors in order to put food on the table for their families.

As enforcement fell off, not everyone was happy with the change. Some people continued to insist that the government not abandon its noble experiment too soon. They argued that it would take an entire generation for the United States to see the actual benefits of Prohibition. They believed that people who grew up under Prohibition were more likely to lead dry lives. What Prohibition needed was more time.

Temperance advocates also pointed out that alcohol consumption rates were at only a fraction of their pre-Prohibition levels. They said that the cost of alcohol was prohibitively expensive for many Americans, and this meant that wages were being more wisely spent on family necessities rather than wasted on drink.

While the logic behind "Their Security Demands You Vote Repeal" may not be obvious now, it was at the time. This message was part of a compelling campaign, whose thrust was to take the alcohol business out of the hands of gangsters and other menacing individuals and organizations. Saloons, once depicted as the scourge of society, now were portrayed as the businesses of our safe, wholesome, and law-abiding neighbors.

Repeal advocates noted the law's darker side. In addition to the steady increase in the number of murders during the Prohibition years, the number of deaths due to drinking "bad" alcohol, or homemade "hooch," was staggering. In the first seven years of Prohibition, there were fifty thousand alcohol-related deaths in the U.S. In addition, thousands more were left crazed, blind, or crippled by bad alcohol.

Repeal: The Twenty-first Amendment

By 1930 Prohibition had again become a hot political issue, but this time popular sentiment pushed politicians toward repeal. Franklin Roosevelt's promise to end Prohibition helped him win the presidency in 1932. Roosevelt kept his promise. He took his first step toward eliminating Prohibition on March 22, 1933, when he modified the Volstead Act and legalized beverages with up to 3.3 percent alcohol.

The Seventy-second Congress of the United States wasted little time in addressing the issue. Only a month after Roosevelt was sworn in as president, the Twenty-first Amendment to the Constitution was proposed in Congress on February 20, 1933; it read:

> Section 1. The eighteenth article of amendment to the Constitution of the United States is hereby repealed.

Section 2. The transportation or importation into any state, territory, or possession of the United States for delivery or use therein of intoxicating liquors, in violation of the laws thereof, is hereby prohibited.

Section 3. This article shall be inoperative unless it shall have been ratified as an amendment to the Constitution by conventions in the several states, as provided in the Constitution, within seven years from the date of the submission hereof to the states by the Congress.

Once again ratification by the states was rapid. Michigan led off with approval on April 10, 1933. Only nine months later the amendment became law when Ohio, Pennsylvania, and Utah ratified it on December 5, 1933. South Carolina rejected the amendment in December 1933, the only state to do so.

A victorious Franklin Delano Roosevelt celebrates his 1932 victory. Within four months the country would be able to toast his victory legally.

In newspaper accounts the day following the repeal, President Roosevelt celebrated the demise of the Eighteenth Amendment and called the illegal alcohol trade that it unintentionally created "notoriously evil." He went on:

> "The policy of government will be to see to it that the social and political evils that have existed in the pre-Prohibition era shall not be revived nor permitted again to exist. We must remove forever from our midst the menace of the bootlegger and such others as would profit at the expense of good government and law and order . . . .
> I trust in the good sense of the American people that they will not bring upon themselves the curse of excessive use of intoxicating liquors to the detriment of health, morals, and social integrity.

The Noble Experiment in America was over.

An FDR pin from the '32 campaign when he ousted incumbent Herbert Hoover.

CHAPTER 2

Prohibition in Vermont

Life all across America changed dramatically when Prohibition took effect on January 17, 1920. Theoretically, anyone who drank wine, beer, hard cider, or liquor—in fact, any beverage containing over one-half of 1 percent alcohol—had to wean themselves from the habit. Brewers, distillers, distributors, and bar owners all needed to find new ways to make a living. In practice, though, many Americans kept on drinking, and the business of supplying illegal alcohol was born.

Because no other nation enacted Prohibition, foreign suppliers became an obvious source for thirsty Americans to tap. Vermont and other border states suddenly found themselves on the front lines of a nascent smuggling industry, pitting rumrunners and revenuers against each other in an often entertaining, but sometimes deadly, battle. Vermont's border with Quebec was a favorite crossing point for smugglers, and a great deal of alcohol came driving, trotting, rowing, railroading, and hiking across the border and through Vermont. Some of the illegal alcohol was for local consumption, but much of it was bound for urban speakeasies in southern New England, particularly in Boston and New York.

Hardship and Smuggling

When Prohibition was enacted, the Green Mountain State was still largely rural. Two hundred twenty-one of the state's 251 towns had populations under 2,500. Only three Vermont cities had populations over ten thousand, which places 86 percent of the state's 352,428 residents in smaller cities, towns, and villages.

Farming dominated the state's economy and way of living during this era; 72 percent of Vermont land was being used for farming, versus the current 21 percent. There were 29,075 farms (versus 5,828 in 1997), with approximately 290,122 dairy cows and 62,756 sheep. Farming was important to the Vermont economy, with the value of the state's crops totaling $48,006,628. The state was already well known for providing markets in southern New England with quality dairy products (milk, butter, and cheese), certified seed potatoes, eggs, apples, turkeys, maple sugar, and honey.

While the farm economy was healthy, farm life was far from easy, with its notoriously long days and little, if any, time off. The state's northern counties were characterized by a particularly sparse population, bony soils, and harsh weather. Dotted with small communities and a tangle of secluded unpaved roads, some traversing the international border, the region was remote even by Vermont standards, and it remains so to this day. Few people chose to weather the long, cold winters, when less than a hundred miles south the climate was significantly milder. But the cold and

Milking time at an early-twentieth-century Vermont dairy farm. Three milkers outside work on stools while the herd mills about. This scene is a far cry from the efficiencies that were being introduced around this time, such as milking parlors with insulated bulk tanks.

Here dairy farmers bring their 10-gallon milk cans to the creamery—perhaps a cooperative—for processing, such as separating the cream, milk, and whey. The man in the doorway near the roof's peak is weighing in the milk.

day-to-day struggle to survive produced an extraordinary resiliency, making residents feel they could weather any storm, natural or man-made.

Money was still a rare commodity here, and bartering was commonplace. Some newspaper advertisements from the period list the cost of goods in terms of the number of eggs one could exchange for the merchandise. With little industry to speak of, most of the area's inhabitants worked the land to survive. Farmers, many of them French-Canadians from Quebec who had fled even more economically difficult times, fought to make ends meet by farming Vermont's rocky hillsides and valleys. Others made their living by logging and milling the region's vast tracts of timber.

There is more than a little truth to the quip that the people living in this rugged territory didn't notice the Crash of 1929 and the subsequent Great Depression because they had lived in Depression-like conditions all their lives. Most had learned to survive by growing food from the land and raising their own meat. People without such means were generally taken care of in some way by their neighbors.

Yet even these tough folks hadn't weathered a storm as severe as the Great Depression, which cut farm incomes in half as commodity prices plummeted, while leaving many expenses—like loan interest, taxes, and farm merchandise—unchanged. While many people endured, just scraping by, others had to drop to levels most Vermonters thought they would never see. People lost their homes, and many hardworking Vermonters found themselves unemployed; some were forced to live in community-run "poor farms," where they had to work for their keep. Other homeless people, too proud to enter the poor farms and unwilling to suffer the

This advertisement reflects how common bartering was in the period.

stigma of living there, instead chose to go door-to-door, offering to work in exchange for room and board.

One of the ways border-region Vermonters found to supplement their meager incomes during the late twenties and early thirties was smuggling, and one of the most popular items of contraband was alcohol, its value having skyrocketed with the advent of Prohibition.

Vermont's Pre-Prohibition "Dry" History

Vermont has struggled with the question of temperance almost since its founding. The young state's population soared in its first thirty years, 1790 to 1820, from approximately 85,000 to 230,000. Also burgeoning was the alcohol business; an 1818 report enumerated over two hundred distilleries in Vermont.

Fearing that the proliferation of alcohol would lead to moral decay, temperance-minded folks, inspired by Maine's example, rallied to put an end to the "scourge of alcohol." The Vermont Temperance Society was formed in 1828, and by 1837 its members were working for statewide prohibition. The group first pressured the state to regulate the sale and distribution of alcohol to the retailers and innkeepers, who thereafter had to be licensed to sell alcohol. The efforts of the pro-temperance camp seem to have borne fruit, as, by 1840, the alcohol business was severely curtailed: Vermont had only two distilleries and one brewery still in operation.

At the January 1844 meeting of the Vermont Temperance Society, movement leaders decided that because of anticipated legislative opposition to more stringent controls on alcohol, they would call for a referendum on the issue at the county level. The Society's campaign slogan was "Let the people decide the great questions that concern the people."

By January 1845 the Society had its victory, though only by the slimmest of margins: 83 votes of approximately 30,000 cast. Pressured by the outcome, the General Assembly responded on November 3, 1846, by passing Act 24, "An Act Relating to Licensing Innkeepers and Retailers." The law called for an annual statewide referendum to be held on Town Meeting day, beginning in 1847. A "Yes" vote meant that county assistance judges could continue to grant licenses to innkeepers and retailers to sell "distilled spirituous liquors, wine, ale, or beer (excepting small beer)." A "No" vote meant that judges could not grant such licenses and that alcohol would only be available for "medicinal, chemical, or mechanical purposes."

The Yes vote won the referendum by a 3:2 margin in 1847, and Vermont became a dry state. The victory was symbolic more than real, as enforcement of the law was often lenient. It was also short-lived. In the 1848 referendum, the No vote narrowly reversed the previous year's outcome. Vermont was once again wet.

This setback reinvigorated the temperance camp, which now also included the Sons of Temperance, the Green Mountain Tribe of Rechabites, and the United Brothers of Temperance. The temperance coalition rallied the Yes vote in 1849 and won by a crushing 12,000-vote margin. Temperance forces didn't let up, and they engineered another resounding win in 1850. Having won three of four referenda, the temperance movement then worked to solidify their gains by urging the legislature to discontinue the referendum and make the "no licenses" ruling permanent law. The legislature agreed, wrote Act 30, and passed it on November 13, 1850.

Buoyed by their successes, Vermont temperance forces again took inspiration from Maine, where an 1851 law banned the manufacture of alcohol—as opposed to simply banning its sale. Once again they effectively brought pressure to bear on the legislature, and on November 23, 1852, the house passed by a single vote (91-90) Act 24, "An Act Preventing Traffic in Intoxicating Liquors for the Purpose of Drinking." The act, which banned alcohol manufacture in Vermont, called for a statewide referendum on the question in February 1853. Vermonters narrowly approved the new law; it passed by only a 521-vote margin, with over 44,000 votes cast. Thus, in 1853, Vermont statutes tightened their prohibition grip as they banned the manufacture of alcohol for use as a beverage. This law was to stay on the books for the next fifty years.

The Anti-Saloon League created temperance societies, such The Lincoln-Lee League. This member's card, dating originally from 1903, includes a signed pledge to "abstain from the use of intoxicating liquors as a beverage."

While prohibition may have been law in Vermont, the state was never entirely dry. Surrounded by wet states and a wet Canada, Vermonters had no problem obtaining wine, beer, and spirits. Furthermore, enforcement of the law was lax, with the law entirely ignored in communities that were so inclined. For instance, Governor Urban Woodbury, proprietor of Burlington's Van Ness House, not only failed to abide by the law privately, but also flouted it publicly by serving alcohol in his establishment. In addition, opposition to prohibition began to arise as Vermont's tourism industry developed. Pro-tourism lobbyists argued that prohibition created a competitive marketing disadvantage: Why would anybody want to vacation in a dry Vermont, when they could vacation elsewhere and openly enjoy a drink?

The movement to repeal statewide prohibition was led by Percival Clement, publisher of the *Rutland Herald*. Clement championed the idea of the "Local Option," whereby each municipality would decide for itself whether to be dry or wet. Seeking the Republican nomination in the 1902 governor's race, Clement came to the convention arguing for the Local Option as a major party plank. When the party failed to support his position, Clement bolted and played the spoiler: Running as an independent, Clement drew enough of the vote to deny Republicans a majority for the first time in the party's fifty-year history.

Following the eventual joint assembly election of Republican candidate John McCullough, the legislature sought to close the party rift by passing on December 11, 1902, Act 90, "An Act to Regulate the Traffic in Intoxicating Liquor." The act authorized a statewide referendum at Town Meeting in 1903, which gave citizens the right to decide whether their town would be wet or dry, and if wet, to further decide what types of alcohol would be available. By only a 1-percent margin, voters chose to make the Local

GRANDPA AND HIS TWO CHUMS.
THE REAL ISSUE
THE HOME OR THE SALOON
(Anti-Saloon League, Concord, N. H.—No. 4)

In this postcard, produced by the Anti-Saloon League, the recipient is warned to guard these two young boys by voting for prohibition: "Home has them. Saloons will want them. A license law means saloons in some town where there are somebody's BOYS."

Option effective in March 1903. Vermont's fifty years of statewide prohibition ended.

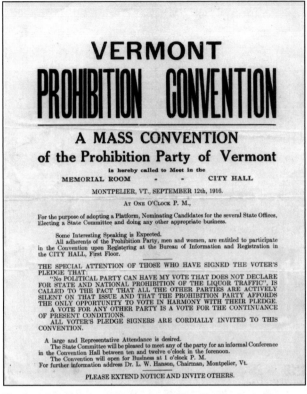

The Local Option became law in 1903, effectively ending prohibition in Vermont, but temperance groups rallied to make Vermont dry once again. The poster above calls sympathetic voters to the 1916 convention of the Prohibition Party of Vermont, at which "Some interesting Speaking is Expected." What this party couldn't achieve at the state level was won on the national level only three years later.

While the Local Option marked the end of statewide prohibition, it wasn't the end of Vermont's temperance movement or Clement's political aspirations. Clement ran again for governor in 1906, this time as a Democrat, but he still lost. He remained active in politics, and was finally elected governor in 1919, when the debate over federal temperance laws was in full swing. Now Clement found himself battling prohibition, this time at the national level. On January 16, 1919, the Eighteenth Amendment was ratified, becoming national law. Once again, Vermont became dry.

Prohibition and Rum-running in Vermont

In a period of only weeks the Vermont back roads leading to and from Quebec were transformed into smuggling routes. Strangers, once an uncommon sight in Vermont's border regions, began to appear: rumrunners. These rumrunners sped through the area, heading north to Canada to pick up alcohol, and then they swept back through with their contraband cargo.

Some of the alcohol coming into Vermont was earmarked for local sale; much more of it was taken to hidden depots and warehoused, where it awaited shipment to southern New England's major metropolitan centers. Lyndonville and Barre were noted for their roles as storage and distribution centers.

Lyndonville exemplifies the less savory and more dangerous side of Vermont's involvement with Prohibition. Located approximately thirty-five miles south of the Canadian border, Lyndonville is now a picturesque college town, but was once a haven for gangsters. A July 29, 1931 article in the *Boston Evening Transcript* described Lyndonville as home to one of New England's biggest bootlegging gangs and a gathering spot for criminals from all across the country.

This advertisement, which appeared in the *Newport Express and Standard* in 1915, reflects then-contemporary attitudes and issues surrounding drinking—attitudes and issues which may seem surprisingly modern.

The ad's reference to "sanitarium time" parallels current reliance on "retreats" and "de-tox" programs. Its promise of "no loss of time from work" mirrors current concerns over productivity losses, also still an issue, as seen in workplace drug-testing.

Vermont's 'Toughest Town' Moves to Rid Itself of Gangsters, reads the *Transcript* headline. A subhead continues, "Lyndonville, Beautiful Village Near the Border, Tires of Being Rumrunners' Hangout—Vigilance Committee Formed." The article warns citizens and readers:

> "They do not realize that among this crowd, at times, are killers, gun men, dope fiends, holdup men, some of the toughest and nastiest of city crooks . . . . Lyndonville is pretty well known all over the country by gangsters, many of whom lay low here in bad times working for the rumrunners.
>
> "If Lyndonville heard someone in Congress not long ago declare that there were more men from Lyndonville in federal penitentiaries, according to population, than from any other place in the United States, it paid no attention."

If Lyndonville residents were complacent, that changed abruptly when four men drove up to the police chief's home in broad daylight, broke into his cellar, and removed a costly load of liquor that the police had seized ten days earlier. "That was the final straw," the article says. Concerned citizens rallied and demanded action, contacting the sheriff, federal prohibition agents, and the state's attorney general. The lawmen joined ranks and launched several retaliatory seizures of their own, including several vehicles used for rum-running.

Fear of crime began to preoccupy the residents of Lyndonville. The sometimes surly and dangerous out-of-state gangsters so worried local bootleggers that they began arming themselves. The business for local bootleggers turned rougher, as rival gangs began hijacking their loads. Instead of risking trips into Canada themselves to pick up a load of alcohol, hijackers laid in wait at night along busy smuggling routes. Seeing a car speeding down the road, the hijackers used a variety of techniques to stop it and check for booze. Some simply pulled their own vehicle across the road, while others more boldly blocked the way themselves, standing in the roadway with guns drawn. The intercepted smugglers, who had only moments before been going about their "business," were abruptly lightened of their loads, and sometimes even their cars. Considering the illegal nature of their work, the wronged smugglers had no legal recourse. Vengeful paybacks weren't unheard of, even here in Vermont, as the wronged outlaw eventually tried to settle the score. Turf wars, once a thing of the cities, had come to Vermont.

According to the *Transcript*, local smugglers were prized for their ability to make the most dangerous part of the trip—getting the alcohol across the border. Thirty miles later they delivered the illegal haul to barns in and around Lyndonville, where it was stored until needed. Rumrunners arrived from such Massachusetts communities as Greenfield, Springfield, and Turner's Falls to pick up the merchandise and bring it down to cities farther south, principally Boston, Providence, and New York.

Rumors of locals striking it rich from rum-running still persist today, and undoubtedly a few Vermonters did make a great deal of money. Evidence suggests, however, that most of the local smugglers were the sort of inconsequential amateurs that the gangsters disparagingly referred to as "small fry." Many made just enough money to help them pay their bills and feed their families.

Most Vermonters were not involved in organized smuggling on the scale that plagued Lyndonville. Ordinary honest folks along the border, most of whom had never been on the wrong side of the law, suddenly found themselves criminals, just for having a drink of beer, wine, or spirits. As a result, many harmless games of cat and mouse developed, as individuals and small-time operators got involved in bootlegging, moonshining, and brewing.

Fact and fiction have become intermingled over the years. Some stories are so fantastic that they are difficult to believe. The newspapers of that era, however, did chronicle many extraordinary events, such as the bootleggers who dressed as priests, hoping to trick lawmen on their return trip from Quebec with a load of alcohol. Inspired, two other men went this pair one better, attempting the same stunt but disguised as nuns.

One account tells of an undertaker who regularly drove a hearse across the border, informing Customs officials he was on his way to pick up a poor fellow who had met his maker while in Quebec. Customs inspectors eventually grew suspicious about the number of Vermonters dying in Quebec, so they opened up the coffin one day upon the undertaker's return to Vermont. Instead of a body, they found the coffin packed tight with bottles of booze. Another smuggler hid alcohol in containers originally made to store embalming fluid.

Lawmen had a variety of tools to combat the relentless and creative efforts of smugglers. While the small-fry smuggler might be detected at the border, professional smugglers generally avoided border checkpoints altogether by using the region's quieter back roads or the remote open waters of the larger lakes, such as Champlain and Memphremagog. Although lawmen improved their chances somewhat with tips from informants who reported on suspicious activities, the modest number of patrols that they could mount placed the odds squarely in the smugglers' favor.

Given that alcohol consumption fell only an estimated 20 percent during Prohibition, vast quantities of illegal alcohol, much of it whiskey and fortified wines, had to have flowed into the United States across its borders. Vermont's share of this heavy traffic is unknown, but the huge volume was only possible because so many professional smugglers were on the roads. These pros ran their business like a freight company, with warehouses, systematic planning, and regular trips. They bore little resemblance to amateurs out to make a few dollars.

When detected by lawmen, the well-financed professional smugglers relied on their best weapon: speed. Driving powerful 12-cylinder Packards and Lincolns, and even 16-cylinder Cadillacs, many smugglers were simply able to outrun the average lawmen. On the water, too, smugglers could afford the fastest transports, choosing high-speed runabouts like Chris Crafts, Gar Woods, and Hackers. Ironically, lawmen only stood a chance of keeping up when they used the vehicles and vessels confiscated from less-fortunate smugglers.

When speed alone was not enough to ensure their escape, rum-runners resorted to a variety of schemes: smoke screens, created by pouring oil on their exhaust systems; hideouts, found by co-opting the barns of more-or-less willing farmers; shooting, in hopes that the bullets would deter their pursuers; and throwing cash out the windows of their speeding vehicles, hoping that underpaid lawmen would be more tempted to stop and pick up the money than to continue the chase.

As Prohibition wore on, pressure began to build for its repeal. Vermonters increasingly voiced their discontent, viewing the law as ill conceived. Governmental resources were increasingly being drained to combat alcohol consumption, with limited effect. High-profile incidents that claimed the lives of small-time smugglers made Vermonters question the heavy costs associated with the law. Expenditures on federal penal institutions increased more than 1,000 percent between 1915 and 1932; even so, penitentiaries were overflowing with prisoners, the majority of whom were incarcerated for Prohibition violations. The Vermont state prison system, including county lockups, was similarly overwhelmed with Prohibition offenders.

The response of judges to this prison dilemma was varied. Some judges simply fined offenders and warned them not to break the law again; others, frustrated by the number of repeat offenders, sent Vermonters off to federal penitentiaries as far away as Georgia. The effects were sometimes catastrophic: Families often became impoverished and were forced from their homes by foreclosure. Because continuous incarceration for three years was legal grounds for divorce, more than one Vermont bootlegger lost his wife and family as a result of his crimes.

The statute also took a toll on society in a more general way, causing the citizenry to lose respect for both law and government. In 1931, Commissioner of Prohibition Henry Anderson warned, "The fruitless efforts at enforcement are creating public disregard not only for this law but for all laws. Public corruption through the purchase of official protection for this illegal traffic is widespread and notorious. The courts are cluttered with prohibition cases to an extent which seriously affects the entire administration of justice."

The Great Depression provided still more incentive for the repeal of Prohibition. The diversion of governmental monies to Prohibition-related expenses versus social services was viewed with growing hostility. The re-legalization of alcohol would, opponents declared, decrease alcohol-related gangsterism and rampant prison and court costs, while dramatically increasing government tax revenues. Estimates varied, but it was argued that repeal would provide one-quarter to one-half million jobs nationally in the business of distilling, brewing, and distributing alcohol.

Deep in the throes of the Great Depression, a growing number of Vermonters were too busy trying not to starve to death to worry about whether or not people drank alcohol. While the state's economy was vibrant in 1920, it was in desperate straits by 1933: of the 350,000-plus residents, 50,000 were unemployed, and of those, only 23,000 were on welfare. Respectable citizens joined the

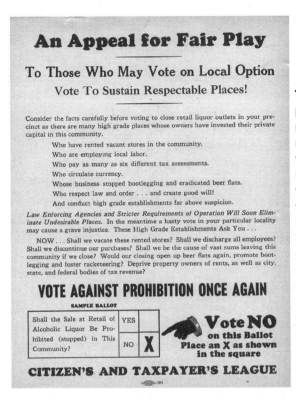

An Appeal for Fair Play

To Those Who May Vote on Local Option

Vote To Sustain Respectable Places!

Consider the facts carefully before voting to close retail liquor outlets in your precinct as there are many high grade places whose owners have invested their private capital in this community.

Who have rented vacant stores in the community.
Who are employing local labor.
Who pay as many as six different tax assessments.
Who circulate currency.
Whose business stopped bootlegging and eradicated beer flats.
Who respect law and order . . . and create good will!
And conduct high grade establishments far above suspicion.

Law Enforcing Agencies and Stricter Requirements of Operation Will Soon Eliminate Undesirable Places. In the meantime a hasty vote in your particular locality may cause a grave injustice. These High Grade Establishments Ask You . . .

NOW . . . Shall we vacate these rented stores? Shall we discharge all employees? Shall we discontinue our purchases? Shall we be the cause of vast sums leaving this community if we close? Would our closing open up beer flats again, promote bootlegging and foster racketeering? Deprive property owners of rents, as well as city, state, and federal bodies of tax revenue?

VOTE AGAINST PROHIBITION ONCE AGAIN

SAMPLE BALLOT

Shall the Sale at Retail of Alcoholic Liquor Be Prohibited (stopped) in This Community?	YES	
	NO	X

Vote NO
on this Ballot
Place an X as shown
in the square

CITIZEN'S AND TAXPAYER'S LEAGUE

This Local Option poster exemplifies many of the arguments supporting the repeal of Prohibition. It points out the positive sides of the legalized alcohol business, including income to the community in the form of rent, wages, and taxes paid. They also tout the idea that their regulated operations help put bootleggers and racketeers out of business.

ranks of rumrunners in order to put food on the table for their families. The difference between eating and starving in a border community could be a fast car and knowledge of the unguarded back roads of the region.

Prohibition's days were numbered.

Repeal and Ratification

Following the passage of the Twenty-first Amendment by the United States Congress in February 1933, states were called on to ratify or reject the amendment. On September 5, 1933, Vermonters voted on a slate of twenty-eight delegates: fourteen pro-ratification and fourteen anti-ratification. Public sentiment was clear: the fourteen pro-ratification delegates received more than twice as many votes as their anti-ratification counterparts. On September 26, 1933 the fourteen delegates then convened in the Senate chamber in Montpelier, where they cast their votes and sent a message to Washington: ratify the Twenty-first Amendment and end Prohibition.

Delegate Walter Fenton addressed the convention, remembering anti-Prohibition activist and governor Percival Clement:

> "Some of us can remember back fourteen or fifteen years when there seemed to be a great hue and cry for the adoption of the Eighteenth Amendment ... and the Senate of that session undertook action to adopt [it].... It was my great privilege at that time to be a part of the official family of a great citizen of Vermont, Percival W. Clement, who had been nominated by the Republican Party for the office of Governor upon a platform the first plank of which was opposition to the Eighteenth Amendment. I recall very vividly an occasion when that gentleman, with the courage which he always possessed, appeared before the Committee on Federal Relations in the hall of the House of Representatives with the room as crowded with people as I had ever seen it, and in a very strong speech pointed out to the persons assembled there and to the people of Vermont, what would probably result if the Eighteenth Amendment was adopted. Somehow or other every one of the prophecies which he uttered at that time came true just as he said they would come true, but they went even further, and conditions developed that no one thought possible or dreamed of under the operation of the Eighteenth Amendment, until the people of this country, disregarding the loud voice of the organized minority who too frequently mistook the echo of their own voice for the voice of the people, rose up in their might in protest against the continuance of such conditions and are now taking out of the Constitution of the United States an article which never should have been put there in the first place. It is a very great privilege to be a member of this convention representing the people of the State of Vermont and to vote in favor of this resolution, and the only regret which I have on this auspicious and historic occasion is that the Honorable Percival W. Clement is not here to witness and participate in the repeal of the Eighteenth Amendment which he so vigorously opposed in his lifetime."

Governor Wilson then addressed the Convention:

"Your meeting here today is breaking new ground in the work of the constitutional law. This is the first time that an amendment to the Constitution of the United States has been acted upon by Vermonters after a popular vote.... I believe that the people of this country are to be congratulated upon finding a way by which the people themselves may determine whether they want an amendment to the Federal Constitution or whether they don't.... The Constitution of the United States should represent the ideas of the people of this country as to the frame of government under which they are to live.... I believe that in these times, when it almost seems as though the constitutional rights of the people are being endangered, here is a salutary event that shows that the people of the country are going to use this great document which is the foundation of our political existence and that they are going to watch it in the future and protect it and that no matter what we may have for emergency measures, we are going to be guided by the Constitution in the end for permanent and lasting government."

Vermont voted to ratify the Twenty-first Amendment, as did, ultimately, every state other than South Carolina. On December 5, 1933, the necessary majority was achieved and the nation, including Vermont, was once again wet.

While Prohibition may have tested Vermont and the nation, Americans and the Constitution withstood the trial. Through the orderly mechanism of government, the Constitution was amended to enact Prohibition, The Noble Experiment. And thirteen years later, using the same orderly mechanism, Americans ended the experiment. Vermonters went about their business, and strangers in the Kingdom were once again a rare sight.

From the distance of seventy years, it is all too easy to regard Prohibition as some quirky historical period, just a collection of facts regarding amendments and statutes. The legalities behind Prohibition provide only the barest outline of what it was like to be alive in this time, experiencing the consequences of these laws.

In the pages that follow, the reader will hear the stories of some of the Vermonters who participated in Prohibition. They include the voices of lawmen and of rumrunners, of citizens watching from the sidelines in small villages and cities, and of citizens dabbling in small-scale moonshining and bootlegging. All the stories have both their humorous and serious sides, reflecting the complexity of life then, as real people—real Vermonters—lived through the era. This book provides a vivid glimpse of that time through the eyes of these spirited participants.

CHAPTER 3

Clarence Morse:
"Good Money in Bad Times"

"Bootlegging was risky business," said ninety-one-year-old Clarence Morse, who doesn't mind admitting that sixty-five years ago he tried his hand at smuggling alcohol. "I did it a few times, but I didn't like it—there were just too many risks. The money was good, especially considering how tough times were, but it wasn't worth dying for," he said, "and some did." Morse said he feels no shame about his brief stint as a bootlegger; he figures he was only doing what was necessary to survive desperate times, and he'd do it again under the same circumstances.

Morse was born on April 19, 1908, in Jay, Vermont, to Herbert and Pearl Morse. He grew up in the neighboring community of North Troy, an Orleans County village bordering Quebec to the north and the Green Mountains to the west. Because North Troy was on one of Orleans County's busiest rum-running routes, the village became a popular stopover point for out-of-town smugglers. Notorious gangsters passed through town, and unsubstantiated stories even have Chicago gangster Al Capone staying overnight in a small North Troy hotel.

Morse is a man with a quick wit and a true gift for storytelling. Coming of age in the middle of Prohibition, Morse said that he nevertheless learned to enjoy having a few drinks, and he and his friends didn't let Prohibition stop them from indulging in that pleasure. They visited some of the so-called line houses, which were unlicensed drinking establishments common along the United States–Canada border, especially during Prohibition, when drinking remained legal in Canada. Many of the houses were entirely in Canada, but others were built right on the line. Though Canadians frequented them, they attracted many American customers as well, some of whom traveled hundreds of miles from southern New England and beyond in a boozy Prohibition pilgrimage. Others, more business-minded, went to the line houses to pick up shipments of alcohol. Some visitors did a little of both.

The nearest line houses in Morse's area were right across the border in Highwater, Quebec. "The Labounty Line House was one of the most popular," Morse said, remembering many trips there with his friends. "The house was split right in two: half was in Canada, half in the States. Some people went there to drink, and many to pick up loads of booze destined for Barre, Vermont, about seventy miles to the south." Morse recalled that Barre served as a depot for much of the alcohol that passed through Orleans County. The alcohol was warehoused there until distributed to other locations in Vermont and throughout New England.

Also in attendance at the line houses were "the moneymen," who worked to entice locals to take the loads for them, according to Morse. "They'd say, 'Can you take a load to Barre?' I didn't bother with them too much. These moneymen were making a

A line house in Canaan, Vermont. This rambling building is typical of many such rough and tumble places, originally built for other functions and often crudely adapted to meet their suddenly increased roles as drinking establishments.

fortune, and the others were taking the chances." Morse said he doesn't know who the moneymen were, but they seemed to be closely connected with the operation in Barre. Local men, who knew the roads well and were willing to drive the contraband, were offered $125 for the journey, a night's work. The trip down took two or three hours—as long as the driver didn't run into any problems with the police along the way.

"That was more money than I could make in three months," said Morse, who, at that time, was making seven dollars a week working on the town's road crew. Times were tough and money was hard to come by. Many people were sorely tempted, and the moneymen used a variety of techniques to win over the reluctant runners, including offering them free beer while discussing the proposition. "They'd get fellows so hot that they'd take a load," Morse said. "A lot of the guys who did it were just trying to make a few bucks to get along. Usually they were just young fellows. They weren't bad people."

Morse related that when he was sober his good sense prevailed, and he could resist their offers; but with each additional free beer, the importuning became more difficult to resist. "Well, the next thing I knew, a couple friends and I were loading up a car with booze." The loads typically consisted of ten cases of beer, Molson or Genesee, and one case of liquor. "At that time a case of beer was twelve quart bottles," Morse explained. The bottles were often carried in burlap bags. No money exchanged hands until the load was delivered. "Back then a man's word was better than anything written on a piece of paper."

Morse said that the cars headed south from Highwater into Vermont, making their way south through Westfield, Waterbury, and Montpelier, the state capitol, before arriving in Barre. This wasn't always an easy task, according to Morse. "Professional drivers knew enough not to drink before a run, because they knew the importance of a clear mind for outwitting the lawmen who lurked in waiting for the alcohol-laden cars flowing south from Quebec. Many of the local boys were too naive to know this, or too chicken to run a load without a few drinks. Many of the people who were caught or crashed did so because of poor judgment brought on by drinking."

Once in Barre, drivers took the cars to a five-bay garage that served as a transfer station. "You had to pull into one of the bays, walk out, close the door, walk into town, and come back in an hour. When you got back to the garage, the load was gone, and there was $125 on the seat," said Morse. "You never met anybody at all. That was quite the business.

"And it was a dangerous business," Morse added. "It was no game." In those days, lawmen could take more extreme measures to stop vehicles than they can today, including shooting out the tires and radiators of fleeing cars. "The greatest danger arose from the fact that not all of the officers were good shots," Morse said. He remembers one rumrunner who was killed during a chase, apparently by accident. The driver attracted the attention of law-men in the town of Jay. "They followed him through Jay and shot him as he was going down the hill into Westfield. They killed him dead. They really didn't mean to kill him; they just meant to stop him," Morse said. That man was Winston Titus and the date was July 20, 1927.

The death was on the front page of many of the state's north-ern newspapers for weeks following the incident. The first papers to hit the newsstands reported that Titus died instantly when his

A group of U.S. Immigration Service officers pose next to a rumrunner's car that they chased and stopped, after gaining the cooperation of its driver by putting four bullets through the vehicle, three into the gas tank.
Lawmen of the era had much greater discretion in the use of their firearms. This chase ended without injury, but others, such as the Titus incident recounted in this chapter, did not. The lawmen too came under fire, especially when dealing with professional smugglers who were sometimes members of out-of-state gang-ster-run organizations.

alcohol-laden car crashed into a tree while he was being pursued by Immigration road patrol officers Nelson Hines and Joseph Faucher. The articles made no mention of any gunshots being fired.

Rumors, however, quickly spread around the county asserting that the "accident" was caused by shots fired by the two officers. The St. Johnsbury-based *Caledonian-Record* ran the following article in the July 25, 1927 issue.

"The death of Winston Titus, a youth under 20 years of age, which occurred in Westfield about 2:20 Wednesday afternoon, is a mystery which federal and state officers are investigating.

The boy, who lived at North Troy, was in a high-powered but old touring car, containing 18 cases of ale brewed in Montreal. Immigration patrol officers gave out a story that he was instantly killed when his car struck a tree and turned over, pinning him under it.

However, it is reported that two bullet holes were found by undertakers in his body, and Mrs. Walter D. Bell, close to whose farmhouse, a mile north of here, the death occurred, heard two sounds which she ascribed to shots fired from a heavy revolver.

The rear curtains on the sides of the car have been stripped off. It was reported this was done by State's Attorney Brownlee, who was soon on the scene, and there is a big hole made apparently by a bullet, about the place where the rear cushion in the car would be. This cushion, it is said, was also carried off by officers.

The Titus boy was of an excellent family of North Troy, and had a good reputation.

Wednesday morning he helped his father in the hay field, and at noon went to the village to have his hair cut and get a shave, and planned to return to work. His father had no knowledge that he ever ran liquor past the border officials. The car which was in this smash-up was bought for a song three days previously at a sale of seized rum-running cars, it is said by George Rolfe, who is reported to be in the liquor business just beyond the line. It is declared that the Titus boy was not an old or frequent rum-running offender. He came across the border, it is alleged, by a rough country road, which a horse and buggy would find difficult, going through North Jay and Jay, and it is reported here that he was being fired at by officers as he went through both places.

Two Immigration officers who had parked a small but specially geared car at North Jay, looking for liquor or immigrant smugglers, ordered him to stop near the line, but he would not. They kept close after him.

Mrs. Bell says that she heard the two cars coming very fast, so fast that she suspected a rumrunner chase, and just after they passed she heard two loud reports, which she feels sure were caused by a large revolver.

The car about that instant struck two trees on a five-foot-high bank about 100 yards below her home, and turned over in the air, falling on its top in the road and crushing Titus frightfully. The right-hand wheels were ripped from the hubs, one of them leaping a wire fence and running 155 feet before stopping.

Officer C. C. Stannard of Lowell, who was passed by the car and its pursuers just in front of Mrs. Bell's home, telephoned at once to State's Attorney Brownlee and to undertaker Jackman of Newport.

Several officers were on the scene within an hour after the boy died.

The Immigration officers who chased him are reported to have been patrolmen Faucher of Newport and Hines of Montreal, the latter a new man in this region who the day before chased and captured a man more than twice his size."

An autopsy on Titus's body confirmed what many people already believed: Titus had been shot—a fact that sent renewed shock waves throughout the state.

The *Caledonian-Record* reported the following in the July 29, 1927 issue:

"The report of the autopsy on the body of Winston Titus, 20 years old of North Troy, who met death while being pursued by two Immigration officers, shows that two bullets went through the boy's body, Attorney General J. Ward Carver announced this morning. 'The autopsy showed,'

Mr. Carver said, 'that one of the bullets entered the back of the boy's head near the brim of his hat and came out the forehead, while the other one entered under the left shoulder blade. Either of the wounds, the doctors claim, would have caused the death.'"

The two officers were arrested and charged with manslaughter. They were each released on $3,000 bail. A grand jury hearing into whether to indict the two officers for Titus's death was convened on August 2, 1927. The findings of the jury were swift and in the officers' favor. After listening to about twenty witnesses, the jurors failed to find evidence to support charges against the two officers.

Mr. Titus's death caused some people to question Prohibition, while others remained staunch supporters. The *St. Albans Messenger* jumped into the fray by writing an editorial that caused at least one other paper in the state to respond:

"Uniformed officers of the federal government again sacrifice a human life in their over-zealous desire to enforce the law.

A citizen of North Troy returning from Canada in his car drives rapidly over the road and is seen by Immigration officers who immediately suspect him of smuggling aliens into this country, so they shout to him to stop and upon his refusal to do so, put after him and in the course of the chase fire at him, his car swerves and hits a tree, and he is removed from the wreckage a dead man.

It may be that the Immigration officers really thought that an alien was illegally entering this country, but an alien alive in this expansive country cannot in any way be as serious as the taking of a human life.

This law enforcement to the extent of taking of life is something that the citizens of the country should no longer tolerate.

The claim that the shooting was done by a young and inexperienced man does in no way relieve the blame on the department. Such things should be impossible. If the new men were given proper instructions at the time that they are sworn in, many of these shooting affairs would never take place.

True, the government does not pay sufficient salary to

attract extra high-class men to the service, but if the service is so vital that human life must be sacrificed on the altar of law enforcement, then the government should either increase the pay or take away firearms from this admittedly inferior class of public servants.

It is long past time that this *opera bouffe* as played along our border be stopped, and if those in charge of border affairs are not capable of enforcing the law with reason and without the loss of life, then they should be removed as incompetent and should be replaced by men who are.

In the meantime, none of us are safe and are liable to meet the fate of Winston Titus at the hands of some hot-headed, cheap boy who has no more brains than to think that as soon as he is sworn in and gets into a fancy uniform with a gun in his band, he is now greater than human life itself. The *Messenger* has been and always will be in favor of law enforcement, but does believe that the enforcement should be made with reason and not by cheap public servants with guns in their hands.

We hope this North Troy case may be tried promptly and thoroughly so that we may know whether or not we have the right to ride along the border without running the risk of being shot by some over-zealous armed officer who thinks that a uniform and badge is a license to take life if his dictates are not followed at once."

Not all editors around the state agreed with those at the *Messenger*. An editorial by the *Express and Standard* in Newport took the St. Albans paper to task for its views of the shooting:

"It is true that the taking of human life is an awful thing. Even when the state takes a life as penalty for murder we shudder. But the question recurs: What method is to be pursued to enforce law?

We who live along the Canadian-Vermont border have been called upon from time to time to witness such tragedy as that which took place on a back road in the town of Westfield last week. An officer of the law, in the course of his duty, is charged with killing a lawbreaker. Should such a thing ever happen? The St. Albans contemporary says, 'This law enforcement to the extent of the taking of life is something that the citizens of the country should no longer tolerate.' Does the *Messenger* really mean this?

A burglar enters a bank, holds up the employees, empties the tills of $25,000, and attempts his getaway. Should an officer in pursuit of the thief use a revolver in an effort to capture him? We submit the question to the *Messenger*.

A neighbor attempts to satisfy an imaginary wrong by setting fire to your buildings. Should an officer who sees the committer of arson attempting to escape use a revolver in an effort to capture the criminal? We submit that question to the *Messenger*.

A fiend in human form attempts rape upon your daughter. Is an officer justified in the use of a gun in stopping the escape of such a lawbreaker? We submit this question to the *Messenger*.

We understand perfectly well that the degree of crime and the circumstances surrounding it often make the result of enforcement, or attempted enforcement, appear stupid or brilliant, as the case may be. But the doctrine that the offender should always be guaranteed safe escape if he has a faster car than the officer, is, in the opinion of the *Express and Standard*, not only dangerous but also stupid. We have heard this preachment of criminal freedom from danger repeated over and over in different forms ever since our border problems, because of new immigration laws and Prohibition, became more numerous and offensive. But we never heard such blanket disapproval of the use of this most effective instrument against aggressive criminality, the officer's gun, before.

Does the *Messenger* really think that the people want no enforcement methods against law breaking which endangers the life of the criminal? Must lawbreakers always be given the 'long end' of the enforcement problem?

Perhaps the *Messenger* has some constructive plan of enforcement which would bring results and at the same time put the lawbreaker at ease while committing offences against the law in so far as endangering his life is concerned. If so, we believe both state and national governments would be only too glad to adopt them, for least of all these governments want to take innocent lives. We have heard this railing against accidents which now and then snuff out the life of one who fails to obey the usual courteous command of an officer, but we have never yet heard a constructive suggestion for its remedy and still leave any teeth in enforcement.

The death of young Titus has not yet been proven to be from the use of an officer's gun. Whether it is or is not such result, his death is unfortunate and untimely, and the *Express and Standard* regrets it exceedingly. But our border problems are difficult ones and need the constructive sympathy and help of people and the press. These problems come under the general title of law enforcement. Too many people believe in law enforcement, but always *but.* The way, or the method, or the means, or the sentiment of the people, or something with the enforcement as attempted is wrong."

Morse said he knew Titus and can still well recall his death and all the commotion that followed. He speculated that the officers probably were trying to shoot holes in the tires or gas tank, located to the rear of the car. Morse believes that the officers accidentally shot high, missing the tank and killing Titus. Morse said the car hit one big tree so hard that evidence of the crash remained at the site for years afterward, including the starter crank, which was originally attached to the front of Titus's car, but was now embedded in the tree.

Morse said he was never shot at during a chase, but he does know what it feels like to have a lawman tight in hot pursuit. "During one run to Barre with two friends, somewhere below Waterbury our Model T Ford attracted the attention of a police officer." The chase was on.

The two cars stepped on it, while Morse and his partners tried to figure out how to outsmart their pursuer. The driver headed down a narrow dirt road, got out of sight of the officer, then unloaded the booze and Morse onto the side of the road, where Morse hid himself and the shipment in the woods. The plan was for the other two men to shake the officer, then return and pick up Morse and the cargo.

"After zigzagging along on the back roads, the driver and his passenger thought they had ditched the officer, so they returned to pick me up." To their surprise and dismay, soon after retrieving Morse and the freight, the officer was tight behind them once again. Realizing that the chances of losing the policeman were slim, and that they had a better chance of escaping on foot, the driver stopped the car. Morse and the other passenger bailed out and ran while the driver, who was too scared to move from his seat, was arrested and jailed.

"They caught him right in front of the statehouse in Montpelier, only a few miles from Barre," Morse said. "We didn't have a car so we went all the way home on foot. It was quite a walk." Another local man later drove to Montpelier and bailed the driver out of jail.

The trips to Barre were always risky, Morse noted, and they seemed especially so after he married Marie Arel and started a family that would eventually number nine children. By the time the country was thrown into the Great Depression in 1929, Orleans County was in straits more dire than it had ever experienced. Nonetheless, Morse had already decided that bootlegging wasn't for him, and he focused his attention on making money legally. "People did anything to find money for food," Morse said. "At one

This rumrunner's car shows bullet holes in the radiator and windshield. While lawmen generally shot to disable vehicles, the uncertainties introduced by shooting from one moving vehicle at another meant that some rumrunners were injured or killed. Rumrunning could quickly turn from a lark, or an impulsive act to make some extra money, to a game with serious consequences.

time during the Depression, I was so poor that I didn't have enough money to buy bullets for my gun, so I used snares to catch rabbits to have something to eat. I was always a guy who worked hard and always found work."

Prohibition was a bad idea, in Morse's estimation. It wasn't hard for most people to get alcohol if they wanted it, and smuggling alcohol was too tempting for those who were desperate to feed their families. "People had to make money any way they could. There was no welfare then, and people who accepted help from the town were called 'town paupers,' a title I was unwilling to accept for any amount of money.

"I could have managed to survive without smuggling, but life would have been a whole lot tougher, and besides that," he chuckled, "sometimes I enjoyed the excitement smuggling brought with it."

CHAPTER 4

Jack Kendrick
"No, Just U.S. Customs"

Smugglers had a problem: Lawmen were increasingly catching on to the tactics they used to take alcohol across the border via the roadways. Given the nature of the business, they soon came up with a solution: They took to the water, including Lake Memphremagog in Newport and Wallace Pond in Canaan. The route that was by far the busiest, though, was Lake Champlain.

The lake's geography—its great size, its many islands, bays, and tributaries, its borders in two countries, and the many communities along its shores—made it an ideal route for smugglers. One hundred twenty-five miles long, the lake stretches from the United States into Canada before it empties into the Richelieu River, which connects with the St. Lawrence River and the Atlantic Ocean beyond. Rumrunners used the lake to smuggle any and everything into the U.S.—from a few bottles of booze to entire barges filled with anything from wine to high-proof liquor.

Canadian brewers and distillers were more than happy to provide their thirsty customers to the south with their products. Foreign manufacturers were no less eager to export to the United States. Ships loaded with foreign-made alcohol unloaded their cargo onto much smaller, privately owned boats along the St. Lawrence River, knowing full well that much of this freight was bound for the States. More than a few of those smaller boats eventually found their way into Lake Champlain and then to population centers along the lake and beyond.

Lake Champlain has two major cities located on its shores—Plattsburgh, New York, and Burlington, Vermont—and each was a regular destination for smugglers. On the lake's western shore is Plattsburgh, a sizable city with a population in 1920 of approximately eleven thousand. The city had plenty of customers for contraband alcohol, and served as home to a major transfer station that handled millions of bottles of booze during the thirteen years of Prohibition. The transfer station was operated by a former college professor who gave up teaching after realizing that the booze trade was much more profitable. Freelance smugglers brought shipments of booze either by land or water to his warehouse, where they were paid in exchange for the alcohol. From the depot, the alcohol was distributed throughout New York state and urban centers in New England.

On the eastern shore is Burlington, Vermont's biggest city, with a population in 1920 of approximately twenty-three thousand. Burlington also had its share of customers and profiteers, who all looked forward to the arrival of the shipments—many of which landed on the waterfront under the cover of darkness.

By 1924, four years into Prohibition, the U.S. Customs Service, realizing that an increasing number of smugglers were using the lake to slip safely through their grasp, decided to fight the bootleggers in their own territory and formed the Lake Champlain Boat Patrol. This small band of waterborne Customs officers plied the lake in boats, usually late at night, in search of smugglers.

Like their land-bound counterparts, the officers on Lake Champlain had to deal with a cunning adversary. Officers needed more than keen eyes—they needed good intuition, because everything on the lake wasn't always as it appeared. They learned to cast a discerning eye over every vessel they encountered. For example, although most smugglers ran the lake late at night, some brazenly came south during broad daylight. What appeared to be a family outing on a sunny summer's day might, in reality, be a smuggler out with his family on a booze run, hoping the sight of his wife and children would throw off any lawmen they might meet.

More commonly, though, smugglers sought to disguise their illegal cargoes as legal goods. To the untrained eye a bargeload of lumber looked innocent enough, but a closer look sometimes revealed that under stacks of lumber were hidden hundreds or even thousands of bottles of alcohol.

Smugglers on Lake Champlain also used "submarines" to bring their cargo south undetected. These submersible contraptions could hold hundreds of booze bottles. Without any power of its own, the sub was towed behind the smuggler's boat. When the boat got underway, the submarine automatically dove and stayed out of sight of the prying eyes of the lawmen—but only as long as they kept moving, for when the boat stopped, the submarine rose to the surface. The sub's drag on the towing boat made it impossible to outrun the boat patrol. Thus, when smugglers were interdicted by Customs agents, they had only two choices: either to accept capture, or cut the sub away and make a run for it, leaving behind thousands of dollars' worth of alcohol.

The men of the patrol had a reputation as a daring lot who loved the water as much as their job. They included Louis Babcock, Laurence Izard, Hugh Lyons, Elmer Palmer, Carl Bashaw, Walter Buckley, Roy Cheney, Eddie Salvas, Fay Templeton, and Armand "Midget" Lavigne, a feisty amateur boxer. A number of college students worked as officers during the summer. One of these was Bradley Soule, who worked for the service during 1924 and 1925, earning $1,680 each season, and then went on to rise to prominence as a doctor at the University of Vermont College of Medicine in Burlington.

The commander of the Lake Champlain Boat Patrol was Captain Jack Kendrick—a charismatic, quick-witted man who wouldn't ask his men to do anything he wouldn't do himself. Writing in 1980, Dr. Soule described his former boss:

> "By far the most interesting [member of the patrol] was our commander, Captain Kendrick, known to everyone as Jack. About thirty years of age, tall, slender, and handsome when I met him, he had a delightful sense of humor and an outgoing personality that made him well-liked by everyone, except possibly the bootleggers."

Although Kendrick has been dead for many years, his memory is very much alive in the mind of Burlington resident Joyce Weldon, one of Kendrick's two surviving children. Joyce spoke passionately of her father and fondly of the crew he led on missions onto the lake.

"He was dedicated to his job," Weldon said. "He took his job seriously, but he didn't take himself too seriously. He was an adventuresome soul who liked to laugh and have a good time. He generally liked people, and, in turn, they liked him. Many people on the other side of the law even became friends, especially after Prohibition was repealed. He believed in service, duty, and sacrifice for his country."

Service was a lifelong affair for Kendrick. At only seventeen years of age, Kendrick set sail for Europe to battle German forces during World War I. Kendrick didn't have to go fight; he joined the effort before the United States was involved in the war. Kendrick signed on with the French Foreign Legion as an ambulance driver, setting out on an adventure that helped shape the rest of his life. After America joined the conflict, Kendrick enlisted in the United States Army and happily served under the stars and stripes of the country he loved so deeply.

It wasn't only patriotism that put Kendrick in harm's way, according to Weldon. He was an intrepid soul who was always eager for a new challenge. Kendrick found in the war both a moral obligation to act as well as a new challenge full of risk and danger.

Kendrick's commanders recognized Kendrick's eagerness and talent. The young man quickly rose through the ranks, and by the time of his discharge shortly after the end of the war, he had achieved the rank of major. But his success came with a cost: When Kendrick returned to Vermont he was not a well man; the war years had taken their toll. Worst of all, his lungs had been damaged by mustard gas, an often-deadly gas that was a favorite weapon of the Germans. "Essentially, my father came home to die," said Weldon.

"My father loved the lake," Weldon recalled, "and he figured if he wasn't going to live a long life, he was going to enjoy the time he did have on Lake Champlain. So, he built a camp right on the lake in Georgia, Vermont."

Contrary to expectation, being back in Vermont seemed to improve Kendrick's health. He wasn't one to sit around and watch life pass him by, so he applied for a job with Customs and was hired. Kendrick found his first assignment as an agent in the rural Orleans County community of Derby Line too boring and isolating. When the boat patrol was formed, Kendrick saw the perfect assignment. He applied and was hired as its first commander.

"The boat patrol was more than a job. It was my father's passion," Weldon reminisced. "He took his post seriously, and he enforced the laws even if he didn't agree with all of them, and one law he didn't agree with was Prohibition." Weldon said that her father and mother, Flora, were sociable people who were invited to many parties, even during Prohibition. "Dad believed in enforcing the law he had vowed to uphold, but when he was off duty at these gatherings, he was known to look the other way. For that matter," Weldon said, "I've heard that my father even enjoyed a drink now and then at these socials."

Kendrick transformed his waterfront camp into the headquarters of the Lake Champlain Boat Patrol. With a long dock and several boats standing by, this facility enabled Kendrick to leap into action at a moment's notice, occasionally recruiting his wife to lend a hand.

Weldon recalls hearing stories about her mother holding a gun on captured outlaws as her father prepared to transport them to the county lockup a few miles away in St. Albans. "That was a bit dramatic for a young woman to be there with a couple of thugs,"

Kendrick and his patrol pose at their lakefront headquarters in 1927. Pictured are (left to right): Carl Bashaw, Kendrick, Ed Salvas, George Horton, Leon Griffin, F. Bedard, Roy Cheney, unknown, and J. Rockwell.

Weldon said. "Mother also knew what she was getting into when she married Dad, and she supported him 100 percent."

Other times Kendrick took his wife and infant son out on patrol with him. "If you think about it, the situation was horribly dangerous," Weldon said, "but he wanted to spend as much time as possible with his family."

Danger was part of the patrol job, and it didn't bother Kendrick. Many of the smugglers were harmless people doing whatever they could to survive the poverty of the times. Another breed of outlaw, however, also traveled the same waterways and roads of Vermont: criminals from urban centers around New England and New York. "Some of the smugglers were hardened criminals with guns, and they were ready to defend themselves," Weldon said. "These guys were nothing to fool with."

More than once the men of the patrol found out just how dangerous some of the smugglers could be when backed into a corner. The following is from a 1932 Customs report:

> While Customs Patrol Inspector Armand L. Lavigne and Customs Inspector Lawrence Izard were maintaining a guard at the motor patrol base located on the Alburg-Rouses Point at 3 o'clock A.M., August 12, 1932, they heard and saw a fast runabout pass through the drawbridge

Kendrick's waterfront camp in Georgia Bay, St. Albans, Vermont, was an ideal location for intercepting smugglers from the north. Kendrick transformed his camp into the headquarters of the Lake Champlain Boat Patrol. Note the various watercraft and a seaplane.

going north and running without lights. They watched the boat, and with the aid of night glasses could see the same and follow its course to a point which they considered would be at or beyond the Canadian line, a distance of about 1-1/4 miles. At this time, there were two men in the front cockpit of the boat.

Having had similar affairs in the past three or four weeks, the officers were very certain that the boat would return soon, probably within half an hour or an hour's time. Knowing that the boat was faster than their patrol boat and being of the opinion that the operator would not stop when signaled, the officers made plans to force the same to stop when hailed.

A three-quarter-inch manila rope was placed across the west channel of the drawbridge, this being the one usually used by them, and the rope was left in such a position that they were in hopes that it would become tangled in the propeller and either stop or reduce the speed of the rum-running boat to such an extent that the same could be overtaken by the patrol boat.

About 3:45 A.M., the boat was heard and seen coming south from the direction of the Canadian line, traveling at a high rate of speed. The boat passed through the west channel of the drawbridge and was some forty feet south of the draw when it slowed down to possibly ten miles an hour for a few seconds, and at this time one of the occupants began throwing out bags containing some merchandise from the boat. The patrol boat immediately gave chase and succeeded in overtaking the so-called rum-running boat, striking the same on its left side with sufficient force to leave some pronounced marks. However, Izard was unable to board it at that time because the driver of the so-called rumrunner struck him with the boathook, which was grabbed by Izard and thrown in the lake.

Shortly thereafter, the patrol boat again struck the so-called rum-running boat a hard blow on the left-hand corner of the stern, and at this time Inspector Izard jumped and landed upon the rum-running boat. As he did so he called out to the occupants, "U.S. Customs. Stop this boat." The two men in charge of the rumrunner were in the forward cockpit, and Inspector Izard went forward to where they were to ensure that his command to stop the boat was complied with, but he was immediately assaulted by the driver of the boat and his companion, Charlie White. At the hands of these two men, he was picked up from the floor of the cockpit and thrown overboard, and the rum-running boat proceeded on its course without making any attempt to pick him out of the water.

The rum-running boat was trailed for some distance by Inspector Lavigne in the patrol boat, who finally lost sight of it. Realizing that he could not overtake the boat, he started to return to his base at the bridge. On the way back, Inspector Izard was discovered in the water, taken on board the patrol boat, and carried to the base on the bridge.

Immediately thereafter, all of the patrol boats on the lake started to search for the rum-running boat in question, which was finally apprehended and seized by me at Vergennes, Vermont, on August 16, 1932. Upon direction of the Collector, the boat is stored with the Champlain Marine & Realty Co. at Burlington, Vermont. At the time of seizure, there was no one in possession of the boat, and no one apprehended with the same at that time.

In a letter housed at the St. Albans Historical Society, Officer Lavigne wrote many years later to a friend and told him what happened aboard their cruiser *X-O* that night.

"Our headquarters was a house on the railroad bridge between Rouses Point and the Alburg shore. We kept *X-O*, *Flopsy*, and a 16-foot outboard boat under the bridge. The cruiser was tied up at the Rouses Point dock.

I'll explain how we acquired patrol boat 4461. At the time I was living in the Windmill Point Lighthouse with my family for the summer. One night, while off duty, I happened to go outside about 1:00 A.M. and I heard what sounded like an old lugger proceeding north in the middle of the lake without running lights. The outboard was pulled up on the shore by the lighthouse, so I paddled it out into the middle of the lake and waited for the return of the boat, which I suspected would be loaded with liquor.

About two hours later I heard a boat coming south from Canada. I started the outboard and took out after it, but the boat went by me as though I was tied to an anchor. The following day, Jack and I were talking it over. He had heard from some people in Rouses Point that a boat had been heard during the night going south from Canada. It always seemed to happen when we were off duty. We decided the smugglers were being tipped off as to our whereabouts. Next to our house on the bridge was a signal tower operated by the railroad. In the tower at all times was a man on duty, who operated signals on each side of the bridge to notify trains when the bridge was clear. We suspected the operator in the tower was warning the smugglers by operating the signals.

Even though X-O was our fastest patrol boat, we still knew we would have to find some way to slow down the suspected smuggler in order to catch it. So we took a 150-foot-long floating rope and coiled it behind our desk in the headquarters house on the bridge. Larry Izard, who was the other inspector working with Jack and I, was living on the bridge. Jack was living at Marn's Inn at the Rouses Point dock where the cruiser was tied up.

We made plans to watch from the bridge where Larry slept on a cot in the office next to the signal tower. I walked out to the house one night, taking precautions not to be observed by the man in the tower. I hid behind the desk in the office while Larry was on his cot pretending to sleep. About 1:00 A.M. I heard someone coming down the stairs in the tower. It was a hot summer night and our door was open. I whispered to Larry that someone was coming, so he began to snore, faking a deep slumber.

The man stuck his head in the door and saw Larry apparently sleeping. He returned to the signal tower and we heard him move the signals. About one hour later, a boat without running lights proceeded north under the drawbridge in the west channel.

When it disappeared in the darkness toward Canada, I took the rope, brought it down under the bridge, and stretched it across the west channel under the drawbridge while Larry was getting dressed. We then got aboard X-O and waited in the east channel for the smugglers to return. The Canadian border is about one mile north, and a short time later we heard a high-powered boat coming from Canada.

We started the engine in *X-O* and waited. The boat came into sight traveling at a high rate of speed and passed under the drawbridge in the west channel and over the rope. Nothing happened for a moment, then after about a hundred yards, it slowed down considerably.

We took after it in *X-O* and pulled up alongside, ordering the operator to stop. Larry attempted to board the boat, which we could see was loaded with liquor. The occupants poked him with pike poles, so I pulled away and then pulled up on their stern at which time Larry was able to step down into the stern cockpit.

Officer "Midget" Lavigne sits aboard a captured rum-runner with the Rouse's Point railway bridge in the background.
Lake Champlain narrows down to only several hundred yards' width at this location, making it a useful control point for monitoring lake traffic.
This vessel is full of burlap sacks, which contain bottles of alcohol being brought down from Canada. The patrol captured many different types of vessels, from this cumbersome launch to small speedboats and full-sized barges.

By this time the smugglers were pulling away as the rope had been chewed up by the propeller and they tried to circle back into Canada. I fired several shots from my .45-caliber revolver across their bow, and they turned and headed south. I followed for about five miles but they had disappeared in the darkness. I turned and headed back to the bridge, and halfway back, traveling slowly, I found Larry unconscious in the water. He was saved from drowning by the life preserver he was wearing.

I pulled him into the patrol boat and took him back to the bridge, where the man in the signal tower helped me bring him into the house and put him to bed until he could be taken to the hospital in St. Albans. Larry later told me that the men on the rumrunner hit him with clubs and the operator said to his companion, "Throw him overboard." We immediately started a search for the boat, and a few days later Jack received a call from the sheriff in Vergennes, Vermont, who informed Jack that the boat we were looking for was anchored near shore on Otter Creek at Vergennes. The boat was seized and taken under its own power to the Burlington dock. The Chris Craft Company claimed the boat due to non-payment of the amount due. At the trial the judge ruled that the boat was forfeited to the government due to the act of smuggling. It was turned over to the Lake Patrol for use and was given the number 4461.

At least one member of the Lake Champlain Boat Patrol wasn't as lucky as Officer Izard. Officer Louis Babcock of Waterbury, Vermont, age forty-two, drowned during the early morning hours of August 17, 1931 during a chase with a suspected smuggler on Lake Champlain. His body was never recovered.

While the details of various newspaper accounts vary, all are clear on one key fact: Officer Babcock lost his life in the line of duty. The following is an account of the incident, in Kendrick's words, as reported in the August 19, 1931 issue of Babcock's hometown newspaper, *The Waterbury Record.*

"The night was clear and calm. The officers were on floating patrol when Babcock and Patrolman Armand Lavigne heard the distant noise of a boat. They spotted an expensive teak cabin cruiser near Sister Island, north of South Hero and off Cumberland Head.

"As the light patrol craft was pushed at top speed to cut off the escape of the cruiser, patrolmen Lavigne and Babcock stretched themselves along the bow of the craft in readiness to board the suspected rumrunner. Striking the heavy wash of the cruiser, the patrol boat was severely tossed about and just as contact was about to be made Officer Babcock was missed. A second later Officer Lavigne succeeded in jumping to the deck of the cruiser and, though unassisted, ordered the arrest of three Burlington men who allegedly were engaged in throwing overboard a cargo of contraband liquor. Meanwhile Kendrick had turned the boat back to go in search of Babcock. He cruised back and forth in the area in which he suspected Babcock, a strong swimmer, had tumbled overboard. No trace of the officer was found."

The Commissioner of U.S. Customs in Washington, D.C. gave his approval to use any amount of money necessary to find the officer's body. Meanwhile, the smugglers were kept in the Franklin County Jail in St. Albans under heavy bail, and their vessel was impounded.

Kendrick and crew continued their search until morning, at which time they were joined by a contingent of other Customs Patrol boats, a boat from the Lake Champlain lighthouse service, and many volunteers, according to newspaper accounts. Ropes with grapples were used in an unsuccessful attempt to locate Babcock's body. Given water depths of about 190 feet and a strong current off Cumberland Head, rescue organizers decided it was too risky to use divers. An aerial search was also conducted, without success.

The *Rutland Herald* paid the following tribute to Babcock:

"It is fitting and proper that due respect and regret be expressed for the death of Customs Patrol Officer Louis A. Babcock, who was drowned in pursuit of an alleged rum-running craft on Lake Champlain. The fact that we may be unsympathetic with some phases of liquor law enforcement ought not to blind us to the courage, resolution, and unselfish devotion to duty shown by some of our own border officers. Officer Babcock died as much a real hero as any man killed in action."

In contrast with the drama of the job when on the water, when winter came and the ice closed, life was much quieter. Kendrick and other members of the patrol occasionally ventured out onto the ice to look for people bringing alcohol down the lake on sleds. Most of Kendrick's time, however, was spent inspecting mail at the Burlington Post Office or checking the bags of railroad passengers. By spring, he was always more than ready to get back out on the lake.

To relieve the tensions of his job, Weldon said her father relied on his great sense of humor. The men even had comical names for a couple of their boats. Their fleet included *Flopsy-Jane*, a long narrow riverboat, and *Old Pops*, an aged forty-five-foot speedboat seized from a smuggler in 1924, and which, after several years of use by Customs, was sold at auction—only to be recaptured in 1932 hauling a large load of beer and wine.

Kendrick and his fellow officers look quite dapper in their dress uniforms sitting along the Burlington waterfront. Seated on "563" are (left to right): Kendrick, Steve Marvin, and Al Crandall. On "4461" are Sed Kelley (l) and Eddie Salvas (r). These two rather fine and expensive boats were very likely confiscated from rumrunners.

Weldon said her father could even find something funny in what could have been a particularly dangerous situation. Smiling, Weldon remembered one of her father's favorite stories.

"One time my father and his crew spotted a rumrunner's boat coming south from Quebec. It was a very dark night and the patrol was able to motor quietly up to the outlaw's boat without the smugglers even seeing or hearing their approach.

"This was much to the surprise of the officers. Under usual circumstances, the smugglers would see the approaching lawmen and a boat chase would then ensue, or the smugglers would try to rid themselves of contraband before the officers boarded their boat, and sometimes they did both, with one man driving while the other was tossing the load overboard. Other times they tried to outrun the officers and hold onto their load.

"But on this night, the rumrunners were completely unaware of my father and the patrol. Without a word, the driver of the Customs boat pulled alongside the smugglers and my father boarded silently. My father, dressed in his uniform of white duck pants and a white shirt, quietly crept forward toward the smugglers, who still hadn't detected his presence. When he was ready, my father snapped on his flashlight and shone the light on himself so the smugglers could see he was an officer. At the same time he hollered 'Stop!'

"The bootleggers looked at him, ablaze in white where a moment before there had been only blackness, and one cried out, 'Jesus Christ!'

"'No,' my father said, 'just U.S. Customs.'"

CHAPTER 5

Sterling Weed
"A View from the Bandstand"

At 101 years old, Sterling Weed, a St. Albans native, had a unique view of Prohibition—from atop a bandstand. Weed has played in the same orchestra, in both Vermont and Quebec, since the very early days of the twentieth century—including the thirteen years of Prohibition. A lifelong non-drinker himself, Weed chuckled that while Prohibition did not change his lifestyle, it certainly provided him with many lasting memories.

Weed didn't play in the line houses, makeshift bars, or other dives along the border during that era. Of the patrons who frequented these seedier establishments, Weed said, "They went to them more to drink than to dance." Seeking a more appreciative audience, Weed and his orchestra played at many of the most popular dance halls and pavilions of the time, in addition to performing at a multitude of musical events held in schools, town halls, and lodges in and around St. Albans.

With more than a century behind him, and who knows how many years ahead of him, this wiry old musician loves to do two things more than almost anything else: play his music, and reminisce about the old days.

With a smile, Weed recalled one of the more raucous events at which his orchestra played. The occasion, held in Morrisville in the early 20s, was a tremendous stag party. Most of the three to four hundred men who attended were World War I veterans, only recently returned from the battlefront.

With five 55-gallon barrels of beer, there was plenty of beer to go around—and then some. "The men had a good time, and things got really wild," Weed said.

"Our playing didn't amount to nothing," Weed chuckled. "I don't know what they had us there for. They didn't know if we were playing or not. They were too busy having a good time."

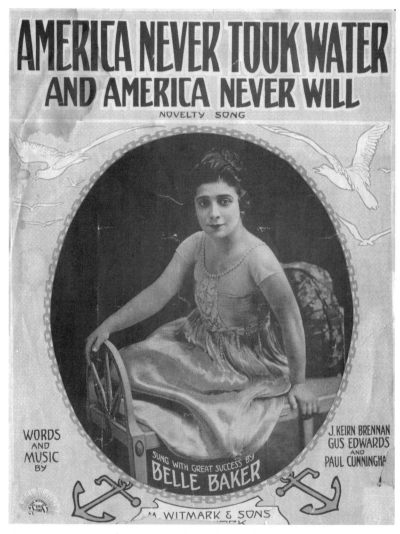

This song, published in 1919, sympathizes with WWI soldiers returning to the U.S. only to be told that they cannot drink. The soldiers complain that they had enough water "in the trenches," and now they'd prefer the drinks they'd been exposed to while overseas: "England gave us ale and porter / To drink their wines, the French taught us how." Notwithstanding, Prohibition was ratified that year.

While lawmen typically enforced the Prohibition statutes, Weed said that they appeared to make an exception for this group of veterans. "People were just too happy to have 'the boys' home to worry about their drinking," he said. "Folks simply figured that after they had served their country and risked their lives, they deserved to drink if that's what they wanted."

Weed was born in St. Albans Town in 1901, one of three sons born into a farm family. He enjoyed a quiet childhood, even as they struggled to eke out a living on the land. A close family, the Weeds did more than work together—they made music together. Both of Weed's parents were accomplished musicians. His father played the violin and trumpet, and his mother the organ and piano. His parents instilled in Weed and his two brothers the love of music. By the time Weed was ten years old, he was playing piano in the family's band—Weed's Orchestra—a group that later, under Sterling's leadership, became known as Weed's Imperial Orchestra. It was the beginning of a musical career that would, amazingly, span nine decades.

On July 20, 2001, in honor of Weed's one-hundredth birthday, the city of St. Albans held a public celebration downtown in Taylor Park. Weed was recognized for his dedication to bringing big band music to the rural farm country of northern Vermont. At the time Weed was thought to be America's oldest active orchestra leader. Weed even received a letter from President George W. Bush and the First Lady, Laura, honoring him on his centennial birthday.

Because he is a living legend in St. Albans, Weed has also been recognized by the St. Albans Historical Society, which has dedicated a room in its museum solely to his life. Housed in the building where Weed attended school, the Sterling D. Weed Memorial Music Room overflows with pictures and memorabilia from his long career.

Weed is a quiet, humble man. He has many opinions and enjoys sharing them, but isn't the type of fellow who forces his ideas on others. Nonetheless, Weed's eyes jump to life when asked to share the convictions and the memories he has accumulated during his 101 years—memories of events that are known to most Americans only through history books. In his youth, for example, Weed played for aging Civil War veterans during Memorial Day services. Ten years later, Weed played when the town was sending its men off to fight in World War I.

Although Weed was born into a family of musicians, he was the first to make a career of it—and a varied career at that. Early on he played the flute, accompanying the silent films shown at the Empire Theater in St. Albans. That job came to an end in the 1920s, when the new technology of talking movies came to town.

Weed also taught instrumental music for several decades in the Franklin County towns of St. Albans, Franklin, Enosburg, Fairfax, and Milton. By his own best estimate, Weed helped educate four thousand young people, some of whom went on to become prestigious musicians or teachers themselves. The number of people who have listened to his music over the course of his career is even more astounding: Weed figures that over one million people have heard him play.

"If I quit playing, I don't think I'd be around much longer," Weed speculated. Music is more than a profession or mere entertainment to Weed—it's his way of life, and his secret to staying young. Although married twice, Weed never had any children of his own. He regards his many students as his offspring.

During his decades with the family orchestra, Weed witnessed the negative effects that alcohol had on individuals and society as a whole. Having experienced life before, during, and after Prohi-

Two musical brothers: Ora (l) and Sterling (r) Weed in 1923.

bition, he feels that he's seen both the good and bad sides of the law. On balance, Weed finds himself on the side of those who pushed for the law in the first place, though he's open-minded about the issue.

"If they want to drink, they can have it, as far as I'm concerned," Weed said. "It's their business. On the other hand," he said, "I really think Prohibition was a good idea. Yes, we had a lot of troubles with it, but just the same, I wonder if maybe the country didn't abandon Prohibition, the National Experiment, too quickly."

From his view on the bandstand he concluded that the law was good for Vermont communities such as St. Albans. Weed remembered that before Prohibition, the crowds who attended most of the dances at which his band played were composed mostly of adults who "weren't afraid to down a few beers," and children were a rare sight.

When Prohibition arrived, the lack of alcohol didn't diminish people's love of dancing, but rather seemed to increase it. Dances became even more popular and turned into family affairs, with husbands, wives, and children dancing all night, largely free from the influence of alcohol.

Weed's Imperial Orchestra, 1932. Weed is seated at the piano.

Weed also noticed another interesting phenomenon during Prohibition: People seemed happier during the Roaring Twenties, a decade famous, or infamous, for free-spirited celebration.

"Oh, there is no doubt people drank during Prohibition in St. Albans and the rest of Vermont," Weed said. There was drinking at some of the dances at which his orchestra performed, but from what he saw, most people drank in moderation and unobtrusively; only a few were brazen enough to drink in plain view of everybody else. Some drinkers kept their bottles under cover, but most stashed their liquor out in their vehicles. They'd have a drink before they went into the dance hall, and would make periodic trips back to their cars during the dance to get a nip.

From Weed's perspective, the good aspects of Prohibition outweighed the bad. "You know, these people who drink—if that damn stuff is out of sight, they forget about it. Yes, being so close to the border, anybody who wanted alcohol could manage to get the illicit drink, but it wasn't always easy to find, and it usually wasn't cheap." These two factors, combined with the risk of legal prosecution, encouraged many erstwhile and would-be drinkers, Weed believes, to steer clear of alcohol.

Across the border in Canada, where drinking remained legal, it was another story. The modest number of drinkers from Vermont was swelled by thousands who travelled many miles from southern New England and beyond. They came by car, bus, boat, and train, passing through Vermont—often St. Albans—on their way to Quebec. The Quebec dance halls that had easily accommodated their pre-Prohibition customers, mainly locals, were no match for the crowds that flooded across the border after 1920. New establishments sprang up following the passage of the Eighteenth Amendment, solely in hopes of making a fortune by satisfying the thirst of American drinkers and revelers.

Weed recalled that some of the Quebec dance halls and pavilions were packed with between seven hundred and a thousand guests. Often there were so many cars that parking lots overflowed, and nearby roads were blocked. "Parking was a nightmare, and sometimes we could barely get the band and our instruments close enough to unload," Weed said. Meanwhile, the frantic dance hall owners struggled to get the busloads of exuberant Americans close enough to disembark.

"The line houses and other establishments that operated for the sole purpose of providing alcohol to customers had their share of problems," Weed said, "and we avoided those rowdy places. My orchestra played the calmer dance halls and pavilions, where the customers' priority was the music, not the alcohol—although many patrons did enjoy a few drinks."

When Weed's orchestra crossed the Canadian border on its way to jobs at favorite destinations in Dunham and Philipsburg, he said that he was forced to leave a large deposit with the officers at the crossing station—roughly four thousand dollars by current valuation. The deposit was designed to help keep orchestras in line

Humorous postcards from the period openly promoted and celebrated Canada's wet status. All along the border, Canadian tourism boomed with the increased number of American visitors.

and out of trouble while in Quebec; after an uneventful night, the deposit was refunded in full as they re-entered Vermont. "This was never a problem for my orchestra," Weed said. "We were there to entertain, not to drink and cause trouble." Weed always got his money back.

"The arrival of outsiders to the St. Albans area, especially on weekends, brought mixed results," Weed noted. The influx of people to the region was good news for businesses and hotels in St. Albans. "Most people behaved themselves; however, there were others who didn't." The county lockup in St. Albans was always packed with people, many of them bootleggers caught while trying to smuggle booze into Vermont from Quebec by car, or down Lake Champlain by boat.

The border crossings were often swamped on weekends, causing traffic to back up. The U.S. Customs stations along the border came to a virtual standstill, even though officers worked hard to keep up with the volume. "There was just an unending line of cars," Weed said.

"I'll tell you what," Weed said. "The Canadians made a lot of money on Prohibition. They built their roads on that. Before Prohibition many Canadian roads, especially those in Quebec, were barely wide enough to accommodate two passing teams of horses," Weed recollected. All that changed during Prohibition, when the roads were widened and paved to accommodate the visiting throngs.

Today, many people who were not alive in those days struggle to comprehend how the government could have possibly won the public's approval to ban alcohol.

"The Prohibition movement in Vermont and the rest of the country was the result of many variables," Weed said. "Mainly, the public was tired of alcohol disrupting people's lives and the communities they lived in." The problems created by the consumption of alcohol were not associated solely with the big cities of America; alcohol was also known to wreak havoc on lives in the backwaters of America, including rural Vermont communities.

Back in those days, St. Albans was prosperous and exciting. Home to several major hotels and a bustling railway hub, the town thrived. "There was plenty of money to go around for everybody," Weed said. But then, as today, there were folks who could turn even good times into bad. Although most men spent their money wisely, others squandered it on alcohol.

Weed told the story of one railroad man in town who made his family's life miserable—a story unfortunately replayed many times over by other men of the era. "The fellow worked all week for his pay, but when he got his check, he'd go right to a saloon and drink his money away," Weed said. "This was a common occurrence before alcohol was illegal." Not only did his drunkenness and frivolous spending cause discord in the family, but it also meant his wife and children were often forced to go without food. With little or no state assistance available, the town found itself responsible for such households. Weed remembers his mother used do what she could to help this family. Many people looked toward Prohibition to cure this scourge; and Weed said that in many ways, it did.

World War I played a huge role in the passage of the amendment, according to Weed. "The U.S. fought the Germans during the second decade of the twentieth century. It was a time to fight America's enemy, not to get drunk," he said. The various groups that wanted to ban alcohol used the war to help promote their agenda. Seeing the growing momentum for national prohibition, Weed said that many politicians threw their support behind the proposed constitutional amendment that would take alcohol out of the hands of Americans. By 1919 the necessary forces had came together, and Prohibition was the law of the land.

Ten years later, the 1929 stock market collapse ushered in the Great Depression, and with its arrival came another shift in people's attitudes toward alcohol. The very illegality of alcohol made it a highly profitable commodity. With incomes falling, the temptation to get involved in bootlegging or distributing alcohol grew. Although Vermonters had learned to survive tough times better than most urbanized states, the Depression proved a tougher struggle than they had previously experienced.

"A lot of people found themselves out of work," Weed noted. "People did whatever they could to make enough money to survive. Some turned to running booze across the border. There were risks in this business, but there was also a risk in not doing it— going hungry."

Even during the Depression, Weed said that money was never a problem for him. Whereas many laborers earned only $10 a week, his salary at the Empire Theater was about $30 a week—

excellent pay that gave him no reason to resort to breaking the law to subsidize his income.

Without the expense of any children, Weed was able to amass about $13,000—a virtual fortune (roughly $140,000 in current dollars). Keeping all that money in the bank proved to be a mistake he would regret for the rest of his life. Weed still cringes over what happened to his savings shortly after President Franklin Roosevelt took office in 1932. The president closed the banks for two weeks as part of a plan to help lift the country out of the Depression. To Weed's profound dismay, his money was all but gone when the bank reopened.

"They took all my money but thirteen cents," Weed said, with as much passion as if he'd only recently lost his savings. "I never got it back. I worked like Hell to save that money, and it all went out the window," he said.

Weed said he'd like to live long enough to have the Democrats give his money back to him, but he is doubtful that will ever happen. With a mischievous look, Weed humorously fantasized about what he'd like to do to members of the Democratic Party for the pain he suffered because of them.

"I'd skin them alive if I could," he said. "I felt like choking the whole bunch of them. Taking a fella's savings is a damn mean thing to do."

In the early 1930s, Americans faced so many problems at home and abroad that, in Weed's view, people stopped worrying about whether or not people drank alcohol. They also grew sick and tired of the Prohibition statutes and the problems they caused. Sensing that a growing number of people opposed the law, politicians started to lean toward repeal. When Roosevelt was a presidential candidate, he vowed to make alcohol legal once again. "Roosevelt kept his promise," Weed said, "and Prohibition was repealed in 1933."

"Some people were happy with the repeal, while others were disappointed. But no matter what side of the issue people were on, they were ready to move on with life, with or without alcohol," Weed said. "Although not everybody drank, many did. Those dances in northern Vermont that had become family affairs during Prohibition reverted back to adult affairs as in the days of old, where children were a rare sight. And once more a greater number of families went without because of alcoholism."

CHAPTER 6

Roger Miller
"Shoe Shine Boys & Fish Peddlers"

Roger Miller of Newport has always been a businessman. A former insurance man and still an active craftsman of one-of-a-kind wooden furniture, Miller got his start in the business world while growing up in Johnson, Vermont. During Prohibition, Miller worked as a teenage shoeshine boy who also peddled alcohol on the side.

Neither ashamed of his short walk on the dark side of the law nor proud of it, Miller has spoken very little about his illegal capers over the years. He said he figured it was better his children knew their father as the good, honest, law-abiding man that he grew into, rather than the curious, ambitious, alcohol peddler of his early years. Now, however, at age eighty-four with all of his children grown, he enjoys talking about those days.

"Prohibition was ridiculous," Miller said. "Tell people they can't have alcohol, and that becomes exactly what they want." In Miller's opinion, the law created a tempting hurdle that people had to overcome in order to get alcohol, and this challenge made drinkers of some who might otherwise never have even tried alcohol.

"Compared to many of today's youth," Miller noted, "most of my teenage friends and I were totally naive about alcohol." There was enough activity in Johnson, however, for him to learn about bootlegging and brewing. He remembers hearing rumors that so-and-so was making money selling liquor or beer. Miller also recalled the never-ending line of booze-laden cars passing through town, coming south from Quebec, and sometimes pursued at high rates of speed by lawmen tight on the tails of the fleeing cars.

"While alcohol may have been illegal," Miller recollected, "getting it was really no big deal for most people. There were plenty of illegal drinking establishments, including one that was blown up when a disgruntled partner dropped a stick of dynamite down the chimney to settle an ownership dispute. Nobody was hurt," Miller said, "but that was the end of that place."

Forty miles to the north was Quebec, Canada, where alcohol remained legal. Miller remembered that this province welcomed alcohol-thirsty Americans. "People from all around New England passed through Vermont to go drink in Quebec," Miller said. Some traveled by cars, others by train. A favorite destination for both locals and visitors was Abercorn, Quebec. Drinking establishments in Abercorn ranged from plush hotels, where tourists could spend the entire weekend, to unsavory industrial buildings. The latter were little more than warehouses where people could load up cases of booze and head back south to the border, hoping to cross back into the United States with their contraband undetected.

For Miller, a trip to Abercorn was a family outing. He remembers the family loading up their Overland automobile and heading north across the border. They didn't ever spend the night. His father would load the car with bottles of liquor and they'd head straight back home, though Miller remembers they'd never know whether they'd make it or not in their unreliable car. What *was* reliable, however, was their success crossing the border; somehow Miller's father never had trouble with the Customs officers on the return trip. While they certainly weren't bootlegging, they

Perhaps just back from a road trip, a young Miller and his father walk across the yard. Miller's father carries glasses and bottles of spirits.

did return with enough bottles to hold his father over until their next trip to Quebec.

His father also brought the family to another favorite drinking destination: Highwater, Quebec. Located just across the border from North Troy, Vermont, Highwater earned a reputation as a town where booze flowed freely and Americans from near and far were welcomed with open arms.

Although Miller grew up with alcohol in the house, and with the not-infrequent sight of outlaws speeding through town, he still had no firsthand experience with it. He remembers the day that he lost his innocence to the world of alcohol. As a twelve-year-old shoeshine boy working in a Johnson pool hall, a local man he knew approached him. The fellow asked whether he'd like to make a little extra money on the side, selling liquor to some of his trustworthy shoeshine customers.

Endowed with a good business sense even at this young age, Miller remembers the first question he asked the man: "What's in it for me?"

The man explained to Miller that he would sell each pint bottle of liquor for a dollar, and from that dollar he would get to keep twenty-five cents. Realizing the potential of making good money in bad economic times—average wages for a laborer then were only seven to ten dollars per week—he quickly accepted the offer, without considering the possible consequences if he should be caught. Miller said, "I was a cautious salesman. I only sold to people I knew I could trust, and I seldom actively tried to sell booze to customers; instead, I waited for them to come to me." The young businessman soon built up a good clientele, which included some of Johnson's most prominent residents.

Seventy years later, Miller still laughs about how his mother, a non-drinker, found out about his sideline business. Tired from a late night's work, the young Miller came home, walked into his bedroom, and undressed, dropping his clothes onto the floor and climbing wearily into bed. Deep in sleep, he was jarred awake by the screams of his mother. His mother had come into his bedroom, and seeing the pants on the floor, picked them up, grabbing them by the ankles to give them a good shaking out before putting them in the wash. When she did, quarters flew out of her son's pockets and rolled all around the bedroom floor. Miller had forgotten to take the pocketful of quarters from his trousers—his booty from the previous night's alcohol sales.

"What the hell are you doing?" his mother hollered. "There's money everywhere. You're making more money than your father!"

Knowing that there was no sense in lying to his mother, the young Miller confessed to his illegal deeds. While Miller's mother tolerated his father's drinking and even went along on the trips to Abercorn and Highwater, she was not about to have a son who peddled booze. "Well, you're going to stop that business right now!" she scolded her son.

"Okay, okay," said Miller, afraid to tangle with his irate mother. Even at that moment, though, Miller knew full well that he had no intention of retiring from his lucrative side business.

"To get hold of alcohol, you didn't necessarily have to buy it," said Miller. "A lot of people around town made their own—and many did so for their own use." What went into these brews? Some were made simply from ingredients people found around them, like the beer made from the sap of sugar maples, or wine made from dandelion greens.

Miller said he and a buddy decided to try brewing beer—not exotic beer, just plain home brew—to pad their pockets with a few extra dollars. Not wanting his parents or the lawmen to catch on to their illicit operation, Miller and his friend hid their equipment deep in the woods.

"There wasn't any one way to brew beer," Miller said. He and his friend brewed theirs in a ten-gallon wooden keg. Little more was needed than yeast, malt, and water, in addition to patience while waiting for the brew to "work." No heat was needed; the yeast fermented at ambient temperatures, keeping the covered keg bubbling twenty-four hours a day for two or three weeks until the beer was ready.

"Everybody claimed they made the best-tasting beer," Miller said, "but I never made such a claim. I thought our beer was nasty. How could anyone drink that stuff?" Miller laughed with a wince as he remembered the taste of his own brew.

The two boys learned to brew beer through trial and error. Miller said nobody could fully appreciate the power of yeast until they had bottled beer prematurely, before the yeast had stopped working. One time, in a hurry to sell a batch of beer, the two boys bottled early, knowing that the beer wasn't quite done. The beer continued to ferment in the bottle, creating so much pressure that the whole lot exploded before they could sell it.

Still vivid in Miller's mind are the swarms of bees, especially the yellow jackets, which were attracted by the sweet smell of the brewing beer. Miller insisted that all a lawman would have had to have done to find their operation was find a bee and follow it long enough. Eventually, the bee would have guided the officer to Miller's small brewery in the woods. It wasn't the law that concerned Miller, however.

"My fear of being caught by my mother was far greater than my fear of being caught by the police," Miller confessed. "By the time I began my illegal brewing, most people, including most lawmen, were tired of Prohibition." Discouraged by the lack of respect the general public had for Prohibition and the lawmen who enforced it, many officers increasingly turned a blind eye to these illegal activities. "Why, some went so far as to work on the side of the law and to dabble in the alcohol trade at the same time," said Miller with mock surprise. "Most officers didn't go out of their way looking for violators," Miller said. "They didn't bother the small-time operators as long as they didn't get too brazen. The feds were another matter."

The federal officers—Revenuers from the Internal Revenue Service—had a different mindset when they made one of their random visits to town. These officers, hired specifically to enforce Prohibition laws, seldom played favorites and weren't prone to turning a blind eye to anybody. The local bootleggers and still operators knew they had to be particularly careful when these men were in town.

"There was a certain showmanship to the whole enforcement game. If the local lawmen made a particularly large seizure, or one they were especially proud of, they'd announce it, and then make a public display of smashing the bottles," said Miller. "But that's all it was—a display. While some of the alcohol was dumped," he noted, "some of it also found its way into the homes of the lawmen, who would either drink it or sell it to their friends to supplement their meager incomes."

Though Miller laughs now as he tells these stories, he said that at the time, he and his friend took the law seriously. The boys did have one close call. Miller's friend and partner, the nephew of a local policeman, overheard his uncle talking about plans to raid a small beer-brewing operation in the woods of Johnson. The friend, realizing the operation his uncle was talking about was his and Miller's, quickly telephoned Miller, saying, "Roger, we're in trouble. My uncle knows all about the still, but he doesn't know it's ours."

The two boys nervously hightailed it into the woods, quickly dismantled their operation, and ran home. Once there, the boys began to relax, thinking they had outsmarted the law. They were wrong. After the lawmen went to the scene and found the operation had been broken down and moved, the uncle confronted his nephew and asked if he was somehow involved in that particular brewing operation. The nephew confessed and braced for the worst. His uncle quietly replied, "Thank you for being honest." He never made mention of it again, and the lawmen never came in search of them.

"People also made liquor," Miller said. "Some people got terribly sick by drinking bad liquor, and others even died." Looking back, these illnesses and deaths come as no surprise to Miller. "People didn't know much about alcohol, really. And there were plenty of myths about how to either purify liquor or test its purity. For example, one useless purification technique involved bread. People thought that if they strained questionable liquor through a loaf of bread, it would remove the impurities."

While this postcard from the period makes light of the dangers associated with making "bad hooch," it was in reality a serious health risk. Over the course of Prohibition an estimated 50,000 people died from bad alcohol. No one knows how many pets didn't survive their owner's botched attempts at moonshine.

Another dubious testing technique involved pouring a small amount of liquor into a spoon, then lighting it with a match. "If it had a blue flame, it was good," Miller chuckled. "There was no sense to it, because there are so many things that burn with a blue flame.

"Prohibition did have its humorous side," Miller said. "For example, the fronts people used to conceal their booze sales operations. The one I remember best was the 'fish peddler' that came to my house." This vendor went from house to house, selling fish. He was convincing enough that he fooled Miller and many of Miller's neighbors. Though it took Miller quite a while to catch on, eventually he did. After the peddler departed, Miller would ask his mother what kind of fish they were having for supper. More often than not, his mother said they weren't having fish at all. This perplexed him. "Why would the fish man stop at the house if not to deliver fish?" he wondered. Finally, he figured out what the fish man was up to—selling booze. Later, Miller learned that the fish peddler also operated a taxi service with a similarly odd twist on doing business. He came to understand why folks would call for a cab and then not get in.

Most of the people in the Johnson area who took part in the alcohol trade—whether running booze across the border or making it themselves—were good people, Miller observed. They were just looking to make a few extra dollars to help them make ends meet, especially during the Depression years following the Stock Market Crash of 1929. "These people weren't gangster types, although big-time smugglers did pass through town, and at least one local man provided them with a place to hide their cars and their stash for a time.

"Few, if any, locals grew rich from Prohibition activities," said Miller. And while breaking Prohibition laws became increasingly common in the period's later years, there were still arrests. "Those who were captured often paid a high price. A jail sentence and fine were tough enough, but many were also unable to make their house payments; while they served their time, they forfeited on their mortgages and lost everything."

Miller doesn't recall any particular fanfare to mark the end of Prohibition on December 5, 1933. By that time he was away at high school, and sheltered from the booze trade. "The end of Prohibition brought at least one change to my family—the end of the runs to Abercorn, Quebec. My father still had to take a little drive, though. After Prohibition ended, voters in Johnson decided to remain a dry town, so my father had to travel to Hardwick, the nearest wet town, to get his booze.

"Looking back on Prohibition," Miller said, "I'd say that in reality, it caused more troubles than it cured. Almost overnight, Prohibition turned many good, law-abiding Americans, including Vermonters, into outlaws. The law encouraged some people to drink, and the repeal of Prohibition took away the thrill, lessening many peoples' thirst for alcohol."

CHAPTER 7

Nelia Spinelli
"Barre's Little Italy during Prohibition"

As a young girl Nelia Spinelli of Barre grew up in the days when many men would leave that community in the dark of night and travel seventy miles north to cross the U.S.–Canadian border into the booze-buying grounds of Quebec. Most of the men returned. Others were captured by lawmen along the way. A few of the men lost more than their loads. They lost their lives.

Barre has a well-deserved reputation as the granite center of the world. The granite, quarried in the adjacent town of Graniteville and finished in Barre, has reigned supreme throughout the world for more than a century, attracting granite workers from many other countries to work in the quarries and sheds that are still in operation today. Many of these workers came from Italy and Scotland.

During Prohibition, this city became renowned for something other than granite when it served as one of the hubs of Vermont's alcohol smuggling trade. States further south, without ready access to the border and the Canadian liquor beyond it, looked north to Vermont—especially to communities such as Barre—to help them quench their thirst for the illicit drink. Spinelli speculated that the granite empire grew as a result of the money generated from the illegal alcohol trade.

The purpose of Prohibition was to make the nation dry, ridding the country of alcohol. "That may have happened in some places, but it didn't happen here," Spinelli said with a wry smile. "Barre was always a wet city." One way or another, city residents who wanted alcohol found a way to get it—whether by making risky trips north to Quebec, visiting a local dealer, or by crushing grapes into homemade wine.

Like most Vermont communities, Barre had its share of temperance-minded folks. They didn't believe in alcohol, and they wanted no part of it. For that matter, they didn't want anybody else to have it either. In the years before federal prohibition, in an attempt to curtail people's alcohol consumption in Barre, members of the local chapter of the Women's Christian Temperance Union established a library. Their hope was that when men got the urge to drink, they'd go to the library and read instead. The WCTU founded the Aldrich Library in Barre, which is alive and well today. An account of the library's history describes how it was founded:

> "Starting with books from a Sunday school collection and a former reading circle, the group formed the East Barre WCTU Library Association in 1910, a time when the women considered drinking quite a problem. Their goal was to start a library to give the men something to do in

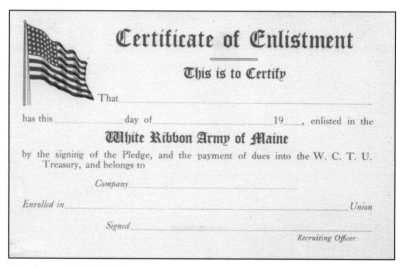

Members of the WCTU joined the "White Ribbon Army." Those who joined contributed financially to the cause with dues and, more importantly, signed the pledge: "That I may give my best service to home and country, I promise, God helping me, not to buy, drink, sell, or give alcoholic liquors while I live. From other drugs and tobacco I'll abstain, and never take God's name in vain."

their idle hours. The firemen built shelves and fixed up a reading room over the hose house. The jail was in the basement, where were lodged those men who patronized the bottle instead of the library. The library hours, six to nine P.M. on Saturdays, may have been planned with a purpose.
"Money was raised by selling ice cream at Saturday night band concerts. In 1916, subscriptions raised in Barre and the surrounding towns made possible a downpayment on the present building. In 1917, after the library was incorporated, the collection was moved to the now-converted space and the tenant took over as librarian for a time. In 1918, WCTU member Louella Pittsley died and left eight hundred dollars to the library."

The anti-temperance forces, on the other hand, argued for the freedom to drink, and even predicted that Barre would suffer financially if the city was made dry. A poster printed during the debate on whether or not Vermont should enact statewide prohibition expressed the feelings of many Vermont granite and marble workers:

"Bear in mind that 90 percent of the granite and marble workers of Vermont are Europeans, and each and every one of them has been accustomed from his early boyhood to take his glass of beer after toiling for hours in the dusty sheds. There is no doubt whatever then, that if the prohibitory law is ratified by the voters of Vermont, most of men engaged in the granite trade will go to the states where they can secure their glass of beer at will. The immigrants will not come to this state when they learn that Vermont is a dry state and that they cannot have a glass of beer after work. Thus it is evident that if the state goes dry, we must all suffer, and trade in Vermont will decrease each year as long as the prohibitory law is in force.
"I make this statement as a skilled marble and granite carver of 27 years' experience, and an adopted son of Uncle Sam. Let us all contribute to the saving of the state from ruination in regard to the granite and marble trade then, and cast our vote in favor of the Local Option Law."

While the prohibition debate attracted advocates for both positions, there is no doubt where Spinelli's vote lies. At eighty-nine years old, Spinelli is an outspoken woman who defends and loves the community that she has lived in all her life. The daughter of Italian immigrants, she takes great pride in her Italian heritage and makes no apologies for those members of her community, especially fellow Italians, who took part in the illegal alcohol trade during Prohibition. She points out that many people involved in the trade did so simply to make ends meet during tough times, or as part of a cultural tradition that goes back hundreds of years.

Spinelli and an octagenarian friend, Antonio (*not* his real name; even now Prohibition's stigma causes some people to speak cautiously about the era) shared some of their memories of life in Barre during the 1920s and 1930s. Too young during most of Prohibition to have participated, neither Spinelli or Antonio took part in the alcohol trade, but both said they were very aware of the illegal activities going on around them—especially Antonio, who lived in Little Italy, the center of the city's illegal alcohol trade.

"There were people in every ethnic group involved in alcohol trade and consumption," Spinelli said, "and the people of Barre's Italian community were no exception." Some were involved in making wine, some in running loads of booze from Quebec, and others just in relaxing with a drink, according to Spinelli and Antonio.

"Italians, especially those from the 'Old Country,' have a taste for wine," Spinelli said. "Wine is an important part of Italy and its culture. There, many people have their own vineyards, where they grow grapes that they crush to make their own wine.

"For most Italians drinking wasn't about getting inebriated," Spinelli said. "They weren't drunkards. They were hardworking people who saw nothing evil about sharing a drink between friends. In Italy they drank wine because grapes were so plentiful and because wine was part of their tradition—a tradition the immigrants brought with them when they came to America."

"Prohibition was a hardship to them," Spinelli said. "Not only was the government telling people alcohol was illegal; it was also essentially telling an entire population of people that their tradition was bad. Whereas most people only lost the right to drink, some ethnic groups, such as Italians, lost a part of their culture that goes back many generations."

Most Italians, like other immigrant groups, came to America in search of jobs. Many who settled in the Barre region were from families that had worked for many generations in the granite trade. Some of the new arrivals and their descendants worked as laborers, blasting loose great blocks of granite in the quarry.

The blocks were then shipped to Barre City, first by truck, and later by train, to the numerous manufacturing plants where skilled workers plied their trades, including sawing and polishing the granite. In the granite sheds highly skilled workers carved the stone into anything from architectural pieces to statues to tombstones.

"The work was strenuous and dusty, and the hours they worked were long and for very modest pay," Spinelli said. "There was little time for fun and relaxation in a granite worker's life, but," she said, "one of the simple joys my father and his friends partook in was playing cards over a few glasses of wine or some other drink. Most Italians, like many other immigrants from Europe, didn't see what they were doing as breaking the law," Spinelli said. "They were just taking part in a tradition passed down from their fathers, grandfathers, and so on.

"That was their form of entertainment in those days," Spinelli recalled. "People today have numerous ways to amuse themselves, such as television and movies. And because of automobiles people can go practically anywhere they want. But back then, all the men had was what they could come up with for themselves. So they played cards, they talked, and they drank."

Spinelli noted that because of the low pay the quarrymen of the early years made, some turned to the sale of alcohol to supplement their incomes. Eventually union rules would help workers receive higher, skill-based payscales, but when Spinelli started working at a granite shed in the early 1940s, a position she held for about fifty years, the workers received a dollar an hour no matter what job they performed. People who carved the granite into various shapes—a highly skilled job—were paid the same as the unskilled workers, who removed waste granite, called grout.

Away from the quarries and stone sheds, the illegal alcohol business offered people a way to make a little extra money, or even big money. There were two levels at which one could be involved in the alcohol business: distributors and dealers.

"At the top of the hierarchy were the distributors," Antonio said. "They hired daring young men, usually in their twenties or early thirties, to drive north to buy alcohol. Then they'd make the dangerous drive back to Barre with hundreds of dollars' worth of booze, all the while staying vigilant for lawmen who patrolled the roads. Back in Barre, the alcohol was put in storage until dealers needed to replenish their supplies. The dealers bought the alcohol from the distributors, and then in turn sold the alcohol to their customers at a profit."

To the best of the pair's knowledge, much of the alcohol brought in by the distributors remained in the Barre area. However, they didn't dispute written accounts of large shipments of alcohol passing through Barre en route to other New England states. They said those accounts could very likely be true, considering that people in those days didn't brag about their illegal activities.

Antonio said that he wasn't involved in the alcohol trade, but he admitted to enjoying more than once the illicit rewards of the bootleggers' runs to Quebec. He said his drink of choice was beer, not the wine that so many of the Italians in those days enjoyed.

"Bootlegging was a dangerous job," said Spinelli, and Antonio agreed. Not only did the bootleggers have to worry about lawmen during their journey home, they also had to be wary of unscrupulous dealers who were always out to cheat the young drivers. Instead of a load of alcohol, all some bootleggers got when they reached Quebec was a good beating, and then they were robbed and sent packing back to Barre with only bruises and a lighter wallet to show for their efforts.

Occasionally the business proved fatal. Spinelli said she remembers at least one Barre man going north for alcohol only to be beaten so badly that he later died from his injuries. She guessed the beating was the result of an alcohol deal gone bad.

"Considering the risks involved," said Antonio, "the smugglers wanted to return to Barre with the biggest possible load. Serious bootleggers didn't fool around with small cars. They used big cars like Cadillacs and Lincolns, cars that could carry hundreds of bottles of booze, much more than smaller cars.

"These cars were so powerful," Antonio continued, "that the only way for lawmen to catch them was to set up roadblocks. Sometimes they stopped the bootleggers during a chase by laying spiked boards in the road. When the outlaw's vehicle passed over the boards, its tires were punctured and the chase was over."

The top priority of the bootleggers was trying not to raise the suspicion of lawmen along their route, Antonio said. Getting caught would mean they'd lose their cars, money, and booze, and more likely than not, their freedom. To make loaded cars look less suspicious to lawmen, Antonio said that the bootleggers, or the distributors who hired them, often had blacksmiths add extra springs to the car's suspension to prevent its rear end from sagging—a dead giveaway that a car was loaded with alcohol. The increased number of springs gave the cars a jacked-up appearance when they weren't in use.

"Smugglers drove under the cover of darkness," Antonio said. "Come nightfall the cars drove out of the garages around Barre, where they were kept hidden during the day, and headed north to such places as St. John, Quebec, to buy alcohol."

For the rough return journey south, the quart bottles of booze— sometimes liquor, sometimes beer—were protectively wrapped in burlap and corrugated paper, and then stuffed in sacks with brand names of legal products on them, Antonio explained. Each bag contained twenty-four-quart bottles of booze. The weight of the hundreds of bottles of alcohol compressed the springs and made the jacked-up vehicles look once again like ordinary cars.

With their vehicles loaded, the men headed south back across the border and on to Barre, hoping to elude the lawmen that prowled the roads. The drivers tried to avoid heavily used routes, choosing instead to use the less-traveled back roads. Some bootleggers went it alone, while others traveled in caravans of two or three cars. The caravan was often led by a pilot car that drove well ahead of the other vehicles, looking for potential trouble. If a lawman was spotted, the driver of the pilot car turned around and warned the approaching drivers to take an alternate route.

Although Antonio wasn't sure of the exact routes that most drivers took, he said that some passed through Morrisville, while others passed along the twisting, and sometimes treacherous, Smuggler's Notch Road that connects Stowe and Jeffersonville. "With a mixture of good fortune and fast driving," he said, "the drivers reached Barre before sunrise, at which time the booze and the cars were put into hiding."

The dealers then bought the alcohol from the distributors. Some of the dealers handled large volumes of alcohol while others sold very little, Antonio and Spinelli said. There were a handful of dealers who made house calls and delivered the alcohol to their customers.

Although most of the bootleggers and distributors were men, there were also many women who sold alcohol. Often these women were widows who sold liquor to help them feed their children. Spinelli said that the Spanish Flu Epidemic of 1918 was responsible for leaving many of these women without husbands. To the best of her recollection, the flu stole the lives of about five hundred people living in Barre. "Whenever there was a death or serious illness in a family," said Spinelli, "a benefit dance would be held at the Union Hall on Granite Street, and the proceeds were given to the family in need. This was a big help to many people."

Antonio said that during that time period many of the men who worked inside the granite shed were dead by the time they were fifty years old from diseases associated with inhaling granite dust, a problem that all but disappeared in the following years after disease-fighting technologies were developed.

"Widows today would be able to fall back on public assistance. That wasn't an option back in those days," Spinelli said. There was little in the way of support from the government, and community support, though heartfelt, was limited. In the end, the women and their children were too often left to fend for themselves. While making ends meet was difficult in good economic times, it became nearly impossible during the depression years of late Prohibition.

"To complicate matters even more for these widows, many of them could only speak Italian, which made finding a job almost impossible," Spinelli said. Many resorted to doing housework for people, hiring themselves out to scrub other people's laundry, and helping women out during pregnancy and immediately after childbirth. Many took in boarders.

"Life was sad for these women," Spinelli said. "They had such a tough life." Desperate for money, some of these widows scraped up enough money to buy booze and then opened their homes to men who wanted to drink and play cards. Tucked away in back rooms, cellars, and attics, these rooms were small versions of what came to be known in the cities as speakeasies.

"Men in Barre were thankful for the widows," Spinelli said. "It gave them a place to drink, hang out with their friends, and play cards. The widows didn't get rich, but they made enough money to pay their bills, feed their children, and continue buying booze.

84

There wasn't any stigma about running such a house because most people realized the women didn't have any other choice," she said. Spinelli also noted that most people weren't in favor of Prohibition. She said her father went to one of the homes just about every night to drink and play cards for a couple of hours, to break up the evening.

To throw off the police and prevent the homes from being put out of business and their operators thrown in jail, the establishments were given fictitious names. The pair chuckled as they remembered the "booze joints" located in "The Meadow," including the "House of the Four Winds" and the "Coconut Grove."

"Men frequented these popular places, where they could get a bottle of beer or a glass of wine and enjoy Happy Hour with friends," said Spinelli.

"Raids by lawmen on these homes and joints were almost inevitable," Spinelli said. Sometimes after hearing about a dealer doing business, lawmen would first send in an undercover officer to confirm the rumors. Once confirmed, the police moved in.

"Not all raids were handled the same way," Spinelli said, "and the outcome often depended on who ran the establishment and whether they could manage to pay off the lawmen. With enough money, the owner could convince officers to overlook their activities.

"The larger dealers, often men, would fork over the money when an officer arrived at their door, and then the officer would go on his way," Spinelli said. The operators were left free to go about their business. Weeks later the police would return to the houses and the operators would pay them off again. It was the price the operators had to pay to keep their businesses up and running.

In contrast, she said, people who couldn't afford what amounted to an extortion payment ended up being shut down, hauled off to court, and often jailed in Windsor. "The cops were crooked. They were corrupt," Spinelli said angrily. "Many of them were just out for themselves. They had no concern for the law."

Other times the lawmen actually raided the wealthy dealers and confiscated their booze. The police claimed that they dumped all the booze in the river, but Spinelli said that wasn't always true. Sometimes they took the confiscated booze and sold it back to the people they had confiscated it from, or they sold it to other dealers.

"The federal revenuers who came from the big cities were a different story," Spinelli said. They didn't play the same games as the local police officers. "These officers meant business. Bribing them wasn't even an option. You couldn't pay them off," she said.

Spinelli said that, to the best of her recollection, the revenuers only visited town a couple of times a year. They quickly learned where booze was being sold, and they too sent an undercover officer into the houses to buy booze. After the officer made a purchase, the revenuers obtained a search warrant and raided the house where the buy had been made. The owners were hauled off to jail, and the alcohol taken.

In a case of mistaken identity, Spinelli said that a judge once issued a search warrant to the revenuers for a raid on her mother's home. She explained that an undercover officer had bought some booze from her mother's downstairs neighbor. To issue a warrant the judge needed to know the name of the occupant of the building. In their research the revenuers came up with Spinelli's mother's name. When the revenuers went to the downstairs apart-

B.G.-48

CLOSED

FOR VIOLATION OF

NATIONAL PROHIBITION ACT

BY ORDER OF

UNITED STATES DISTRICT COURT

———— DISTRICT OF ————

All persons are forbidden to enter premises without order from the UNITED STATES MARSHAL

U. S. MARSHAL

This dreaded sign was the stern evidence of a successful raid by federal agents, "revenuers." While local lawmen might be more lenient about enforcing Prohibition, the "feds" generally lacked any compromising local ties and resultantly were more apt to prosecute the law vigorously.

ment, they quickly learned they had made an unfortunate mistake. The revenuers asked the woman if she was Mrs. Spinelli. The woman explained to the lawmen that they were at the wrong apartment and that Mrs. Spinelli lived upstairs.

The revenuers knew they were at the apartment where the sale had been made, but there wasn't anything they could do about it; because the warrant had been issued for the wrong person, it was invalid. To make matters worse, Spinelli said the local newspaper got wind of the search warrant and inaccurately reported the raid on her mother. "Mother wasn't very happy with the publisher," Spinelli said, "but the paper refused to recant the story."

Smuggling wasn't the only way people in Barre got alcohol. Many families made their own wine. Grapes weren't illegal during Prohibition, but winemaking was. Many Italian families in Barre had grapes shipped in by the train carload. These families, who would never otherwise have considered violating a law, picked up their portion of the grapes and set to making wine.

Antonio and Spinelli outlined the process. The winemaking began with crushing the grapes to extract their juices. The grapes were typically crushed three times. A high-quality wine was produced from the first use. A lower grade, and less tasty wine, was made from the second squeezing. Then, on the third and final use of the grapes, the skin and crushed pulp were squeezed again, the juices fermented, and the resulting alcohol distilled into a potent form of liquor called *grappa*.

"Grappa is a very, very strong liquor," Spinelli explained. She keeps a bottle of Italian-made grappa in her house to give a visitor a pick-me-up or make special drinks. "Most people do not drink grappa straight but put it in coffee, making a coffee royal," said Spinelli.

Prohibition didn't officially come to a close until 1933, when President Franklin Roosevelt upheld his campaign promise to abolish the statute. Following Roosevelt's election in 1932, Spinelli and Antonio said that the federal government began to ease up on enforcement. First beer was allowed, and then other forms of alcohol followed, they said. Some restrictions remained: Alcohol could only be sold during specified hours, and it could not be sold at all on Sundays.

"When Prohibition ended, you can't believe the number of beer gardens that opened in Barre—practically one on every corner of

Main Street. They did a big business until such time as it was legal to sell in stores again," recalled Spinelli.

After the official repeal in 1933, residents of each community in the state were given a choice about whether to stay dry or go wet. "There were many communities that decided to remain dry for several years after the official repeal," Spinelli said, "but whether you lived in a dry town or a wet town, people had little trouble getting their hands on alcohol."

CHAPTER 8

Egnas Limoges
"On the Smugglers' Route"

It was the early 1930s and Egnas Limoges, then a strapping young French-Canadian farmer in his twenties, was doing his farm chores by hand as he did every day. On this day, however, he noticed a car broken down near his barn, which stood beside the main road from Newport, Vermont, to North Troy and the Canadian border. Although the road was a major smuggling route, Limoges was a trusting man; it never crossed his mind that the fellows standing next to the car might be up to no good. And being a good Catholic, he would never have intentionally helped someone who was breaking the law.

Limoges, now ninety-six and living in Newport, recalled that one of the men walked over to him in a bit of a hurry. "This guy said, 'Can I bring my car over? It's broke down.'"

"The fellow seemed a bit nervous, but I didn't hesitate to lend a hand," said Limoges. He hitched up one of his horses, thinking he'd simply tow the car off the road and into his farmyard. But that wasn't what the two men wanted; they were interested in his barn. Limoges observed that they were clearly jumpy about approaching cars, as if they were trying to hide something. The two men finally cajoled Limoges into allowing them to put their car in the barn. Limoges swung open the two big barn doors and the three men, helped by the horse, rolled the cumbersome automobile under cover. Once inside the barn, the two men did something that convinced Limoges they were definitely on the run: They hurriedly swept away any tracks leading into the barn and then banged the great doors shut.

Quietly Limoges peeked inside the car, something he hadn't bothered to do while hitching up the horse, and he saw exactly what they were trying to hide—a carload of booze, probably picked up just over the Canadian border in Highwater.

"Bootleggers or not," Limoges said, "I wasn't about to send the men away with a broken-down car. Besides that, they really didn't seem like bad guys; in fact, they seemed like everyday, ordinary fellows." While the bootleggers appeared anxious about being parked in the barn of a man they didn't even know, Limoges was uneasy about having them and their load of booze in his barn. Times were tough enough; the struggling farmer had no interest in compounding his problems by being arrested for harboring outlaws.

Limoges went about his chores while the two men tinkered with their car for several hours. Finally, at about nine that evening, the car roared to life. Under the dark of night, the men swung the barn doors open, handed the farmer a five-dollar bill for the use of his barn, and then sped off into the night. As Limoges watched the two men head south, he found himself wondering where they were headed. Although he didn't support what they were doing, part of him hoped they'd make it there safely without attracting the attention of the lawmen.

A few days later, Limoges was reading the newspaper and spotted an account of a police chase that had occurred twenty-five miles south, in Barton, Vermont. The story recounted a valiant attempt by a couple of rumrunners to avoid capture—an attempt that failed when they eventually fell into the clutches of the pursuing officers. The captives were the same two who had stayed briefly with Limoges.

"I was sorry afterwards that I'd let them use my barn," Limoges said. His sense of sorrow didn't stem from a feeling of guilt about helping others break the law, but rather from sympathy. "I still find myself wondering about it; if I had refused them help, well, maybe they wouldn't have ended up sitting in the Orleans County lockup."

Limoges, now a retired farmer and still a devout Catholic, recalls the Prohibition years as a time when the morals and beliefs of even the most God-fearing men were tested. "The times were so tough, and the law made so little sense, that many people abandoned their beliefs for the quick money that bootlegging offered.

"I had a hard time, but I never lost my faith," Limoges said, as he told of the temptations he faced, first while living in North Troy, and later in Newport Center on the farm he and his wife, Rachel, owned. Limoges is proud of the fact that, other than the time he unintentionally assisted the two stranded bootleggers, he managed to stay on the right side of the law throughout the Depression, a time of great poverty that challenged many Vermonters.

Farmers and their barns were some of the smugglers' strongest allies. The barns—large, dark, and cavernous, with their big doors—were perfect hiding places for booze-laden vehicles and their drivers as they leapfrogged down the state. Smugglers often knew farmers along their smuggling routes who could be persuaded to give them a place to hide their cars. Other times, especially when being pursued by lawmen, they'd bargain with any farmer that they came across, trying to talk him into the brief use of his barn. When things got really hot, some brazen smugglers simply opened the barn doors and pulled into the barn without first seeking permission. They knew there was considerable risk in doing this—such as facing a shotgun in the hands of a cantankerous farmer who didn't appreciate trespassers. For the outlaws, some of them carrying guns themselves, the risk was worth it—especially when they had lawmen on their tails.

While Limoges didn't let bootleggers use his barn other than the one time he was fooled, he still encountered evidence of smuggling. He chuckled about the time he found a burlap bag full of booze bottles on his lawn. Limoges guessed that some smugglers who were being chased tossed the bag out the window to dispose of the evidence as they fled. "Some people would have smashed the bottles. An even smaller group would have turned them over to the proper officials," said Limoges, laughing. "But I did what the majority of people would have done if they found themselves in the same predicament: I drank it."

The years have been good to Limoges. A tall man with a heavy French-Canadian accent, he is in remarkable health. Blessed with a memory as sharp as a man half his age, Limoges is a walking Vermont history book.

Born on October 10, 1904, in St. Marcel, Quebec, Limoges moved to Vermont as a boy before World War I with his siblings and parents, Lewis and Virginia Limoges. His parents had failed at farming in Quebec. After a brief stint working at the mills, Lewis and Virginia moved the family to a farm on the Missisquoi River in North Troy. Like many other French-Canadian families, the Limoges came to the States to escape the poor economic conditions that were gripping southern Quebec, where the situation was even bleaker than Orleans County's own lackluster economy. The Limoges family joined many other French-Canadians in North Troy. "Many of these families still live here today," said Limoges, as he rattled off surnames common to Orleans County, such as Therrien, Dubois, Tetreault, and Boudreau.

"Times were not easy in the States, but they were far better than in Quebec," Limoges recalled. "Vermont's economy was already weak, and then along came the Stock Market Crash of 1929. It sent the U.S. economy into turmoil; milk prices tumbled, putting farmers like me in a financial bind," Limoges said. "The Depression had a terrible effect on farmers and other country folks, but most Vermonters still had it easier than people living in large, urban centers around the country. Vermonters, especially those living in the north country, were used to hard times, and knew how to use the land to help meet their needs."

In addition, Limoges said that Vermonters knew they could lean on their family and friends in difficult times. "City folks often weren't as lucky," said Limoges, pointing out that most didn't have the land to raise their own crops and meat, and many didn't have a close-knit family to rely on during the tough times. "Country or city, though, during the Depression more than a few people lost everything, and people from all walks of life found themselves living on town poor farms, one of the only forms of public assistance at the time," said Limoges. "Because of the stigma associated with these farms, people usually did whatever was necessary to avoid calling one of them home."

To many people experiencing economic woe, smuggling alcohol across the border seemed like the perfect way to alleviate their suffering. Farmers, especially those along the border, were no exception. Some turned to smuggling, while others willingly opened their barns to bootleggers. While there wasn't as much money in the latter, the risk of getting caught was much lower than for those running the booze.

A humble man, and never one to seek the spotlight, Limoges said that like his father, he has tried to lead an honest and clean life because of the blessings God has bestowed on his family. He thanked God that after his mother died in childbirth, his father was fortunate enough to find a good woman to marry and help raise his children as if they were her own.

The Great Flood of 1927 convinced Limoges absolutely that God would help lead him through tough times. The flood was one of the worst natural disasters ever to hit Vermont. Striking on November third, it wreaked havoc in the state, washing out bridges, homes, and businesses. Property damage was estimated at $300 million (in current dollars). Floodwaters claimed eighty-five lives and left an additional nine thousand people homeless.

When the flood hit, Limoges was safe in the village of North Troy where he lived, but the waters left his parents and siblings battling for their lives. The Missisquoi River rose to nearly unimaginable heights, and moved his parents' home off its foundation. The first casualties were the farm's livestock, all of which were swept away and drowned. That tragedy past, the family then became worried about their own safety. Limoges's parents became increasingly nervous as the water, after flooding the cellar, entered the ground floor and began to climb the stairs.

Retreating to the second floor, the family watched the water continue to rise, now nearly reaching the top of the stairs. Desperate, the Limoges family climbed onto the porch roof and tried

This photo shows State Street, in Montpelier, on November 4, 1927, the third and final day of the eight-inch rain that caused the vast flooding. Water is seen flowing rapidly down the street, having risen half-way up the first floor of the buildings. All the state's northern rivers overflowed their banks at record levels. Montpelier was inundated by the Winooski River, just as Limoges' family was struck by the Missisquoi.

everything possible to attract the attention of would-be rescuers. The elder Limoges rang a bell and shot a revolver, but nobody heard the noise or the family's desperate cries for help. Little did they know that the young Limoges and his brother were in the process of an unsuccessful attempt to reach the house.

Realizing there was nothing anyone could do for them now, Limoges's father placed a statue of Saint Anne, the Virgin Mary's mother, on the head of the stairs and began to pray for God to stop the floodwaters from rising any further.

His prayer was answered.

The rising water came no higher. There is no doubt in Limoges's mind that it was the hand of God that saved his family. Eventually, they were all rescued. "My father was crying when he saw me," Limoges said. "He didn't think he'd ever see me again."

Limoges said his father, and the good, moral upbringing his family provided, helped keep him out of trouble, but he joked that he was simply too much of a chicken to get involved in the risky business of bootlegging. "I didn't want to get caught. I had a good name, and I didn't want to ruin it," he said. It wasn't that he thought drinking was bad. On the contrary, he enjoyed a drink now and then; it's just that he felt obligated to follow the law even though he didn't believe it was right.

"Back then there wasn't much for entertainment in the county," Limoges said, "and people were a lot busier than they are today." Work took up most of their waking hours, although basketball was one favorite leisure-time activity, Limoges said. Every town had a team that competed against the other town teams in the region. There were also dances that people held in their homes.

Limoges insists the French were the ones who really knew how to have a good time. "The English thought they needed a dance hall to have a dance, but the French knew better," Limoges said. "All we needed was a room in a house, a fiddle, and a little spirit. We called them kitchen junkets. All the furniture was removed, and the fiddler brought the room to life as people square-danced the evening away. There was very little drinking at these dances.

"Basketball and dances weren't enough for some people, though," Limoges said with a wry smile. "The bars and line houses in Highwater and other Quebec border communities tempted many across the border." On more than one occasion, the temptation proved too much for the young Limoges. On these outings he and his friends set off across the border on horseback.

"I never drank to where I didn't know nothing," Limoges said. "I'd share a quart of beer with a couple friends." Being firmly against overindulgence was one reason Limoges gave for not drinking more, but the cost of beer was another factor. "As best I can recall, a quart bottle of beer cost twenty-five cents, which was about an hour's wage at the time.

"Those border bars and line houses generated a lot of business from the States," Limoges said. People came from as far away as southern New England and usually stayed for an entire weekend of drinking. "Most of them were half drunk when they went back, and there were a lot of accidents," Limoges said. "At least when my friends and I went on horseback," he chuckled, "the worst that could happen was one of us could get drunk and fall off his horse."

The cross-border traffic kept Customs officials on their toes. It was customary for the folks who visited the bars to try to sneak some booze past the officer on their return trip back into the country. Some officers tried to catch every bottle; others were known to turn a blind eye to the fellow who simply wanted to bring home a bottle or two. They chose to focus on the "real" smugglers who loaded their cars full of booze and headed south.

Not many of the true smugglers were brazen enough to drive their loaded cars right through Customs. Most skirted the Customs stations by using unguarded back roads. Fearing he didn't have what it took to be a successful smuggler of any sort, Limoges said the only alcohol he brought back to Vermont with him was the alcohol he had consumed.

Prohibition was repealed in 1933, when Limoges was almost thirty years old. "It was repealed none too soon," he said, "and the repeal took a lot of drivers off the roads, especially ones that had been drinking." The passage of the Twenty-First Amendment to the United States Constitution repealed national prohibition, but it didn't necessarily make alcohol legal. States and communities had the option of establishing their own alcohol laws, and some chose to remain dry. While Vermont went wet, it allowed each community the right to adopt its own laws on the issue.

For several years following the repeal, Limoges's hometown of Newport Center remained dry. Limoges remembers that the drive to prohibit alcohol was spearheaded by members of the community's Advent Church. "They didn't believe in drinking— it was as simple as that," he said. Remaining dry, though, didn't set well with the folks in town who were happy to see the national ban repealed only to find they still had to travel several miles to "wet" Newport to buy alcohol. "The way this group looked at it, the town was losing money because a few do-gooders were forcing their beliefs on others," Limoges said. "Those in favor of allowing the sale of alcohol in town believed that because people were going to buy alcohol no matter what, they might as well buy it in Newport Center and keep the money local."

Limoges said he helped rally other members of the sizable French population to turn out in force at the next vote. The organized French vote was enough to topple the town's prohibition on alcohol, and Newport Center became wet. "People deserved the right to choose whether or not to drink," Limoges said. He said he has never been a big drinker, but admitted that it was nice to be able to go to the nearest store to get a drink and not have to make the journey—whether by horse or by car—down the smugglers' route and across the border into Quebec.

CHAPTER 9

Percy Daniels
"Murder & Mayhem,
Rum-running & Romance"

Prohibition brought death to the tiny Essex County logging town of Norton, and Percy Daniels remembers well the day that his neighbor's boy was shot and killed by a notorious outlaw.

"The young man's name was Rene Malloy. He was a lively kid," Daniels recalled. "And Norton, being a small town—well, everybody knew Malloy and his family." His death shocked both the family and the entire community.

Daniels, ninety-seven years old, said rumors claimed Malloy and a couple of other men had gone to Quebec to buy a load of booze from a big-time smuggler by the name of Albert St. Pierre. During the trip, something went terribly wrong. When the shooting was done, young Rene was dead and his brother wounded. St. Pierre turned himself in, but the court showed no mercy. He was tried, convicted, and hung in Sherbrooke, Quebec. The following article appeared in the December 22, 1931 issue of *Palladium and News*, North Troy, Vermont's local paper.

"Albert St. Pierre of Hereford, Quebec, was found guilty Thursday afternoon of murder, after three hours of deliberation by the jury following his trial in Sherbrooke. St. Pierre was charged with the killing of Rene Malloy of Norton Mills on November 11, 1930, and has been sentenced to be hanged on March 18, 1932.

St. Pierre's execution will conclude a diversified career, which earned him the cognomen 'the Al Capone of the North Country.' During his reign as a liquor baron, he ruled his mysterious rum activities with an iron hand throughout northern Maine, New Hampshire, Vermont, and the Province of Quebec. 'Line-bound' when he escaped from the county jail at West Stewartstown, New Hampshire, St. Pierre fled into Canada and made his home at Hereford, Quebec, a few miles from the international border, and continued his activities until the night of November 11, 1930, when the Dube farm, where he stored his liquor, was visited by Rene Malloy, his brother, Philip, and a friend, Joseph Langlois. On that Armistice night was enacted a gun battle, which resulted in the death of Rene Malloy and the injury of his brother who escaped after a perilous trek to his home ten miles away."

St. Pierre was eventually hung in May of that year. A May tenth article in the *Palladium and News* reported the execution.

"Albert St. Pierre of Hereford, Quebec, convicted of the murder of Rene Malloy of Norton Mills, ascended the scaf-

The Half-Way Hotel, also known as Pierre's Place, a line house in Hereford, Quebec, not far from the U.S. border. Rene Malloy may have gone here, or to a similar place to pick up alcohol on the evening he was fatally shot.

fold and paid the supreme penalty at Sherbrooke, Quebec, Friday morning. Exactly at 5:05 o'clock, as the first streaks of light appeared on his last day on earth, the trap was sprung by hangman Arthur Ellis. Fifteen minutes later the body was cut down and pronounced dead by Dr. J. E. Daignault, jail physician, and the end of justice had been met."

Daniels, a retired fishing guide and one-time logger and farmer, known for his dry sense of humor, reminisced about the old days when men like St. Pierre thumbed their noses at the law and ruled the North Country with their own brand of justice. Daniels constantly nursed a cigarette as he spoke, occasionally taking a short drag. He started smoking when he was very young, and joked, "If cigarettes killed you, I ought to have been dead ten years ago."

Norton is a community of about two hundred people in Essex County, and is located within one of Vermont's largest tracts of forest. Immediately to the north is the Quebec border, and the New Hampshire border lies less than twenty miles to the east.

"Norton was pretty important at one time," Daniels said. Back in the 1920s, with nearly double its current population, Norton boasted two sawmills, two stores, and one hotel, with another hotel across the border in Stanhope, Quebec. Prohibition brought a lot of people and action to the area as people traveled to and from Canada where liquor remained legal.

Daniels is blunt about his opinion of Prohibition. "It was the ruination of the country, especially for these border towns," he said. "The law brought trouble and troublemakers to Norton, mainly folks on their way to Canada. Most passed through peacefully, but others insisted on creating a disturbance as they went. Worst of all, the law suddenly turned law-abiding local residents into outlaws. Before Prohibition," he said, "people living in Essex County were too busy working, many of them in logging camps, to have time to break any serious laws. With the arrival of Prohibition, some town residents got their first taste of the wrong side of the law.

"Prohibition caused a great controversy on the border," he added. "People who wanted to drink, drank. Nobody paid much attention to the law. And because of a loophole, people often drank openly. The law only prohibited the manufacture and distribution of alcohol—it said nothing about drinking it. The lawmen couldn't do anything about drinking per se; they could only take your liquor away from you. That's all they could do."

Daniels said he knew many people, including some friends, who smuggled alcohol. Most of the locals involved in smuggling were just trying to make an easy dollar. "I'll tell you what happened: There would be a man who had a big family, and all of a sudden he'd be wearing a new suit of clothes and be smoking a big cigar and not working. Why? Because he was smuggling liquor. Some made big money in the liquor trade. Most, though, barely broke even. And others went to jail and lost their shirts."

Smuggling cows, not alcohol, was the only smuggling Daniels did back in that era. "At one time, you could buy a cow for fifty dollars in Canada and bring her over here and sell her for a hundred." By smuggling the cows, farmers could also save themselves the expense of the veterinary exam required when importing cows legally into the United States. Daniels smuggled the cows through the woods during the dark of night to avoid the watchful eyes of Customs officers.

"I knew of a guy who had fifty cows coming down the road, and they caught him. He lost the cows, he lost the money he paid for them, and he paid a fine. Total that up, and the guy lost a lot of money." Though cow-smuggling was illegal, Daniels rationalized the difference: People smuggled alcohol to make money, but people smuggled cows only to *save* money.

Most people bought their alcohol in Coaticook, Quebec, fifteen miles north of Norton. "It was easy to buy," Daniels said, "but getting it back into the country was a different story. Some people never got caught, while others ended up in jail, some on the first try." There was little chance of getting a good-sized load of alcohol past the Customs officers at the border stations, so bootleggers either risked speeding across the border on unguarded roads, or brought their shipments through the woods on foot, carrying bottles of alcohol in burlap bags on their backs. Others used horses to carry the loads through the woods. "Smugglers took the horses a short distance into Canada, loaded bags of booze onto them, and then went back across the border leaving the horses behind," Daniels said. "A short while later, the horses usually followed. You can take a horse twenty miles from home and he'll come back."

Once the horses arrived on the U.S. side of the border, the owners unloaded the bags and quickly hid the bottles of booze, in case a lawman had spotted and trailed the horses. The method worked well, Daniels said. Sometimes the horses were caught and seized along with the alcohol, but the smugglers were usually a safe distance away. "Losing the horses wasn't typically a big deal," he said, "because most smugglers were wise enough not to risk losing good horses making the journey." Instead, they relied on worn-out, tired old horses that struggled under the weight of their illicit cargo. Even when the horses were captured, recovering them was relatively easy and cheap. Because Customs officials didn't want the expense and bother of taking care of these hungry, scrawny captives, they would quickly put the horses up for public sale to the highest bidder. More often than not, it was the horse's original owner who paid the price to reclaim it—putting it right back to work plying the woods along the border.

The railroad passes through Norton on its way to Island Pond, where the lines continued on to Boston, Massachusetts, and Montreal, Quebec. Freight cars were popular with smugglers, both big-time and small-time, Daniels said. Nobody knows how many freight cars loaded with bottles and barrels of booze managed to slip by the eyes of the federal officers, who could only randomly

In rural areas such as Vermont, one of the smuggling vehicles of choice was the horse. Here Canaan, Vermont Customs agents hold five horses that were captured on a mountain trail entering the U.S. from Hereford, Quebec. The horses are heavily burdened with burlap sacks full of bottles. Their owners were not spotted, but probably had been monitoring the horses' progress from a safe distance when the lawmen arrived.

101

check the cars before they crossed into Vermont. "Without a doubt," Daniels said, "at least as many got past as got stopped."

People traveling back to the U.S. by train after a weekend of drinking in Quebec also tried their hand at bringing alcohol across the border—not by the carload, but by the bottle-load. Daniels noted that the lawmen weren't very interested in these folks. "Most only had a bottle or two. If the inspectors found somebody with a little alcohol, they'd usually take it away and send the offenders along, short their booze," Daniels said.

One regular rail passenger had a unique way of smuggling small amounts of alcohol, according to Daniels. "She carried what appeared to be a baby, but in reality was a hollow doll made of rubbery plastic. While in Canada, the woman filled the baby with alcohol. As far as I know, the woman cradling this ever-quiet infant never attracted the attention of the officers," laughed Daniels.

"You heard lots of interesting stories about Prohibition goings-on," said Daniels. "It wasn't always easy to know which were factual and which were more the stuff of folklore."

Daniels recalled a story about two Customs officers who decided the federal government wasn't paying them enough. They subsidized their income by going to Coaticook for lunch during the week. While there, they loaded the trunk of their car full of alcohol and drove back to work, later selling their shipment for a tidy profit. "Nobody bothered them at the border because they were American Customs officers," Daniels said. They got away with it until Customs caught on to their scheme and sent a special agent. "He put an end to the men's lunchtime capers. They lost their jobs in a hurry."

Two lawmen smash confiscated bottles of alcohol. While such displays were commonplace, they were often for show. Estimates generally conclude that only 5 to 10 percent of the alcohol passing through Vermont was seized; these seizure rates are comparable to national figures.

Along with the amusing smuggling schemes, there were many humorless affairs that concluded with graver consequences. The February 6, 1926 issue of the Newport *Express and Standard* reported the death of a former Customs officer-turned-smuggler during a booze run:

"Augustus F. Lawrence of Bennington, Vermont, and Greenfield, Massachusetts, was identified as the man who was fatally injured between Windsor and Ascutneyville late Sunday night, when the automobile in which he was riding sideswiped another car while traveling at a high rate of speed. Lawrence was a former member of the U.S. Customs border patrol. During Lawrence's service as a patrol officer, Hilda Stone was active in rum-running, and for irregularities during his term of office and suspicions that he was linked up with the 'Bobbed-Hair Bandit,' his resignation was requested, effective January 1 of this year. Lawrence had twice served as a Customs officer. He received a temporary appointment on August 1, 1924, and served until October 15, 1925. He was appointed again in 1925 and served in Quebec City, Montreal, Alburg, Vermont, and finally with the border patrol at Beecher Falls, Vermont.

According to records at Customs headquarters, Lawrence was born in Vergennes, Vermont, on December 30, 1902. Subsequent to his discharge he was engaged in the rum-running business, as was proven by his arrest by the border patrol in North Stratford, New Hampshire, on May 2, when he was stopped and his car was discovered to be full of choice liquors, such as scotch, gin, rye, wine, and ale—270 bottles in all. He was released after furnishing bail of $800, and his case was to have been heard soon in New Hampshire Federal Court.

The automobile that caused his death Sunday night was also found to be transporting a load of wine and beer.

By these two instances and other circumstances known by men engaged in patrolling the border, the charge that Lawrence headed one of the biggest rum-running operations this season appears to be well-founded. No less than five cars from his rum fleet have been seized this season. The vehicles demonstrated Lawrence's disregard for the health and safety of his former fellow officers, as each was equipped with an apparatus to generate a smoke screen. This fatal accident occurring when Lawrence was engaged in rum-running, while he was also facing one charge in federal court and had accrued numerous other offenses, justifies the apparent lack of official sympathy for Lawrence. One official simply cited the epitaph appearing on a tombstone in Newport's Pine Grove Cemetery: *Here lies one who will never again engage in rum-running.*"

American agents were not the only ones who were tempted by Prohibition's lure of easy money. An article in the December 24, 1920 issue of the *Newport Express and Standard* tells the tale of two prominent Quebec men who ran afoul of the law in the Vermont border community of Holland in Orleans County. When stopped, their car was found to contain seventeen cases of whiskey and ten gallons of "high wine."

"U.S. Customs officers Rice and Lockland of Derby Line, assisted by Deputy Sheriff Cosby, made a seizure in the town of Holland on Wednesday, in which prominent Canadian men figured. Attorney Cabana of Sherbrooke, who loses his Ford car, and J. H. A. Gemest, the bailiff of Sherbrooke, are in Orleans County jail under heavy bail for smuggling Canadian liquors into the United States. Both men were jailed on $1,000 bail."

The article goes on to say that the bailiff had taken the license number plate from his own car and put it on the Ford owned by Cabana. Although the liquor is said to have cost the men about $500, it is estimated that the trip would have earned them about $2,200 upon delivery to Berlin, New Hampshire.

Whether legal or illegal, there has always been a lot of traffic across the Vermont–Quebec border, and many friendships and families link people on both sides of the line. "People in Norton and surrounding communities have always looked to Quebec for entertainment," Daniels said. "Norton is at least thirty miles from any Vermont community that has any kind of real entertainment. If you want to have a good time, you go to Canada; it's natural to just go on up." People today still go to Canada, because while the drinking age in Vermont is twenty-one, it's only eighteen across the border. Daniels mused, "I think young people have been going to Canada to drink probably as long as there has been a border to cross."

Daniels recalled how, as a young, single man, he and his friends would either take horses or vehicles up to the line houses or hotels in Quebec. Their favorite watering holes were fourteen miles east, just over the line from Canaan, Vermont. In good weather, it took about an hour to get there in a Model T Ford, Daniels said. During the winter and mud season, however, the roads weren't passable at all by car. "Now you can make the trip in ten minutes," he said with a laugh.

"The line houses were fun places to go," he said, although he insisted that he drank very little. "If you wanted to have a party and a little to drink, you'd go across the line to a hotel. You could stay overnight; you could stay for a month if you wanted, as long as you paid your way. People from down-country would come up here for a weekend and just have a good time."

This self-promotional postcard of the Canaan Line House notes its location as Canaan, Vermont and helpfully offers travelers the opportunity to "Stop for Information." This message overlooks perhaps its most attractive aspect for many visitors: the establishment straddled the international line, and alcohol was legal in the Canadian portion of the building. Sharp-eyed readers may notice that the Canadian flag includes the Union Jack, as it did until the new national (Maple Leaf) flag without it was adopted in 1965.

Daniels mentioned one more reason to go to Canada: making new friends. He paused, leaning back for a moment in his chair, and smiled. "You know, it was on one of those trips that I met my future wife, Ethel Markwell, of Baldwin Mills, Quebec." The contented expression on Daniel's face seemed to indicate that he was very glad he made the journey.

CHAPTER 10

Garnet Harvey
"Chases, Wrecks, and Hideouts"

Garnet Harvey of Enosburg said that the border patrol and Customs officers of the 1920s worked diligently to catch their man, and they often did. The only problem was, sometimes they caught the *wrong* man—like the time they apprehended local farmer Victor Couture, mistaking him for a smuggler.

"Couture was a big man," Harvey said. "To me in those days, he looked about seven feet tall, and he was about as rugged as they come." Couture was so mad he scared the Customs officers, who were already embarrassed enough about their mistake.

"Mister, if you've ever seen a mad Frenchman, it was him," Harvey said. "He called them everything. Boy, I can hear him swearing now!"

Harvey, a well-spoken man in his early eighties, laughed as he outlined the events that led to the Couture fiasco in front of his parent's farm in the Franklin County border community of Berkshire.

Given the town's population of only six hundred people, Harvey said that his father knew everybody in town, including the local Customs officers, who were in the habit of stopping by the house to sit around and share stories of their exploits on the road. As a young boy, Harvey enjoyed listening to the officers' tales of the late-night chases that pitted them against the outlaws. While not all of the officers agreed with Prohibition, they all believed in carrying out the job for which they were hired.

Early one morning while Harvey and his father were in the barn milking their forty cows, two officers pulled into the yard, got out of their car, and walked into the barn where the father and son were at work. The three men chatted while the young Harvey eavesdropped on their conversation.

The officers told his father they had been tipped off that a smuggler was likely to pass by the farm that morning. Suddenly, Harvey said, they all heard the loud sound of a car fast approaching from the direction of the Canadian border, only three miles north of the farm.

Young Harvey ran to a window with a good view of the road. "I could hear this car roaring down the road," recounted Harvey. The officers excitedly scrambled back to their own car. "As they ran," Harvey continued, "one of the officers said with some satisfaction to the other, 'Oh, we're gonna get this one!'"

Reaching their car, the officers pulled out what looked to Harvey like a four-foot plank. When the officers carried it to the road, Harvey saw that it hinged open to create an eight-foot plank bristling with 20-penny spikes. Having deployed the device across the narrow dirt road, the officers dashed behind some nearby bushes to await their prey.

"The roar grew even louder, and this car came through like a bat out of hell," Harvey said. The car ran squarely over the spikes, flattening all four tires. The officers, thinking they had gotten their man, jumped out from their hiding place and ran toward the car that was now limping to the side of the road. Before the car had even halted completely, however, they realized they had made a terrible mistake: The driver wasn't a smuggler—it was merely Couture on his way to work.

Couture jumped out of the car, his face already red with anger. After a quick look at his four ruined tires, he turned on the approaching officers and let loose a tirade that Harvey had no trouble hearing from his position at the barn window. Peace was eventually restored when the contrite officers promised to buy Couture a full set of new tires.

More than seven decades later, Harvey, formerly Berkshire's longtime town clerk and state representative, said the Couture incident is only one of many in which innocent people found themselves caught up in Prohibition's battle against alcohol.

The years have been good to Harvey, who lives with his wife Dorothy in the village of Enosburg Falls, a short distance south of

Berkshire. Harvey was born in 1916 in Dunham, Quebec, to Oscar and Lillian Harvey. His family moved to Berkshire in 1919 in search of a better life.

When reminiscing about the old days, Harvey regularly reminds his listeners that his stories, while entertaining, are completely accurate. Harvey's keen memory brings the tales to life, and convinces his younger listeners that some surprisingly exciting events did indeed occur in their now apparently sleepy community.

Victor Couture wasn't the only one to have a legitimate complaint against the lawmen. One time Harvey's father's wrath came crashing down on them. Harvey said his father walked to the barn early one morning and found the big doors to the hay barn wide open. His father was mystified, knowing he had left the doors tightly closed. Investigating, he found evidence that Customs officers had opened the doors, backed their car into the barn, and hid there hoping a smuggler would happen on by.

"Dad had a lot of respect for officers and he valued their work," Harvey said, "but he didn't want to be known as a man who helped them do their job." Angry, he called the Customs office and demanded to know why the officers had been in his barn without his permission. "I'll tell you right now, we're going to have some trouble," his father scolded over the phone.

During the conversation Harvey's father learned that the regular Customs officers were on vacation, and substitutes from New York were replacing them. They didn't figure Harvey's father would mind if they hid inside his barn. "Apparently things were different in New York," Harvey explained, "because in Vermont, most farmers didn't look kindly on anybody into their barn—especially without their permission."

This photo, labelled "Looking for Whiskey, Derby Line," shows soldiers along with lawmen and citizens. While the atmosphere seems casual and friendly, the presence of militia in homeland operations reminds us that this was a "war" on alcohol.

109

"I don't mind you catching the rumrunners," Harvey's father told the customs officials, "but I *do* object to having you back your police car into my barn." He was also concerned that the heat of the exhaust would ignite the hay chaff littering the floor and burn down the barn.

The smugglers, for their part, pressured people not to help the police. "Those outlaws weren't skittish about using threats and intimidation to shut up people who were too friendly with the lawmen," Harvey said. He recalled the story of a Berkshire woman who lived on a major smuggling route and acted as a snitch for the officers. She kept them abreast of smuggling activities on the road.

One day, two men paid her a visit. After confirming she was the woman they were looking for, one of the men suddenly stepped back, pulled a camera from underneath his overcoat, and took her picture, Harvey said. "The man then gave her a veiled threat: 'I understand you've been passing information on to the officers about our activities. I hope this doesn't happen again.'

"She was scared," Harvey said. "That was the end of her reporting."

Harvey's family had more than one run-in with smugglers. The most unsettling encounter was the time a group of smugglers hid two cars behind the family's shed, out of sight from the road. He and his father discovered the cars while on their way to bring the cows in for milking. The drivers weren't anywhere to be seen, so Harvey and his father went to the shed to investigate. "Seeing the cars was surprise enough," Harvey said, "but we got a bigger surprise when we opened the shed door and found two men standing there holding sawed-off shotguns.

"I'll tell you, they were ready for a battle," Harvey said, "but Dad wasn't the type of man to back down during a confrontation. He wasn't afraid of the devil himself. He commenced to chew out the two outlaws: 'What the hell are you doing on my property? You've no business being in here!'"

Facing the elder Harvey's wrath, the smugglers apologetically explained that they had been involved in a police chase earlier that night and had pulled in behind the shed when they realized they couldn't shake the officers.

"My father looked right at them and said, 'I am not going to be a party to this business. I'm going after my cows. When I come back, I want those vehicles gone, and I want you gone. I don't ever want to catch you here again.'" When the father and son returned, the cars and the men were gone, but sitting near the door was a gallon of booze of the type that his father referred to as "highwine." The men had left it as payment for use of the hiding place and for not turning them in. The family never saw the two men again.

"Prohibition and alcohol were not much talked about at home," Harvey recalled. "In 1924, when I was eight years old, I began to learn about smuggling, alcohol, and the law. My whole family was sitting on the front porch to witness a solar eclipse that darkened the midday sun. Suddenly, a big open four-door automobile came to an abrupt halt in front of the house. A man jumped from the car and said 'What the hell is going on? It's getting dark at two in the afternoon!'"

Harvey's parents calmed the fellow, and he sat down with them. Noticing that the car's door was still wide open, Harvey's mother directed her son to go shut the door before another car came along and ripped it off.

"I remember the look of near terror on the driver's face as I started to head for his car. When I got to the car, I noticed a tarp covering the backseat. As I closed the door, I snuck a look under the tarp. To my amazement I saw many bottles stacked one on top of the other."

After the fellow had said his farewells and driven off, Harvey's father explained that their visitor was a rumrunner with a load of alcohol. From then on, Harvey said, the smugglers always fascinated him.

"One morning I woke up to find a demolished car sitting in the highway within thirty rods of my house," said Harvey. "The car had failed to negotiate a corner and had slammed into a stone wall. Of course, in typical kid fashion, I had to go down and find out what was going on. The whole front of the vehicle was shoved in. Broken and unbroken booze bottles were scattered all over the place. I can see the bottles now."

Harvey said no smuggler was in sight, but tracks suggested that the fellow had set off on foot across the family's meadow and kept right on going. Eventually, Customs officers arrived on the scene, collected the bottles, and had the car hauled away. To the best of Harvey's knowledge, the rum-running driver was never caught.

Harvey was in high school in 1933 when Prohibition was repealed. "In effect, though," Harvey said, "it was repealed in 1932 when Franklin Roosevelt was elected president and promised its repeal, because enforcement of the law virtually ceased at that point." Harvey wistfully recalled the impact of the repeal on life around town: "The roads around Berkshire suddenly became much quieter and less exciting. The chases ended, and the rum-runners dried up and disappeared."

CHAPTER 11

Warren "Jersey" Drown
"Confusing Times for Children"

"Life during Prohibition was filled with mixed messages," said Warren "Jersey" Drown of Newport. His mother was a firm believer in Prohibition, yet many other Vermonters treated the law with skepticism, and regarded some of the better-known smugglers as folk heroes who flouted the U.S. government and its agents.

"It was a confusing time for a young man trying to make sense of right and wrong," Drown said. "On one side of the law was my mother, a prohibitionist to the core. Like your toughest cop, she saw no middle ground." Yet, Drown also remembers wondering why, if alcohol and smuggling were so bad, so many people were drinking and risking their lives and property to acquire just what the government said they couldn't have—alcohol.

Every community has a "Jersey" in their midst: a man everyone recognizes and most know by name, even if they have never met him. This old forester, although in his eighties, still refuses to quit working, and he continues to employ his quick wit to bring the history of Vermont alive for its younger generations. Drown said that he likes to see people laugh, especially young people, because as a boy growing up in the depths of the Depression, he had little to laugh about.

Drown has lived in Newport, a city of about five thousand, all his life. In fact, he and his wife, Gertrude, live in the house he grew up in. The road that passes by this house served as one of Orleans County's busiest smuggling routes during Prohibition.

"When I was growing up, you were supposed to know right from wrong," Drown said. "And if I ever became unsure about which was which," Drown laughed, "my mother, whom I loved dearly, was very much ready to steer me in the right direction. Dad had strong beliefs, too," Drown continued, "but he was usually wise enough to keep those beliefs from Mother."

While Drown's mother was a "staunch prohibitionist," seriously opposed to alcohol in any way, shape, or form, Drown's father didn't concur. "He wasn't so sure about the wisdom of Prohibition, but he pretty much kept these thoughts to himself, especially when my mother was around. Under her influence, I grew up thinking Prohibition was a good idea."

Chases between rumrunners and lawmen offered free entertainment—but you needed to be quick enough and wise enough to move out of the path of the speeding vehicles, many of which shot past his front door. The chases captured the imagination of Drown and his young friends, all of whom wondered what went through the minds of the outlaws as they fled the pursuing police. Though law-abiding themselves, Drown said that he and his friends admired the men who challenged the law.

Newport, the state's northernmost city, was a bustling railroad community during Prohibition. The logging industry and numerous mills rounded out area payrolls, providing much-needed jobs in this harsh and difficult climate. Fishing also employed many people, both directly and indirectly. Newport was known for decades as a salmon-fishing mecca that lured fishermen from far and wide.

Main Street, Newport, Vermont, circa 1920.

During Prohibition, the city attracted more than fishermen; it attracted bootleggers in droves from all over New England. Adding their numbers to those of the homegrown Vermont smugglers meant that lawmen had their hands full. The local Orleans County lockup—a small, brick structure that still stands today—had many guests. Some were members of the unfortunate minority that fell victim to good police work or simple bad luck, such as breaking down when their car was loaded with bottles of contraband liquor.

The Drown family also owned a farm on Lake Road on the outskirts of town. Lake Road wends its way along the shores of Lake Memphremagog, from the heart of Newport to the U.S.–Canadian border six miles north. Memphremagog means, in Abenaki, *big waters*, an apt name for this international lake that stretches thirty miles from Newport, Vermont, to Magog, Quebec.

For hundreds of years before the arrival of European settlers, the Abenaki used Lake Memphremagog for travel. During Prohibition the lake served as a major route for bootleggers, and even today it continues to function as a preferred route for smugglers bringing in drugs and illegal aliens. The lake bottom is rumored to hold many bottles of booze, a few liquor-laden boats, more than

The little-changed Orleans County Lockup today. Located just off Main Street in Newport, this jail became home to many unfortunates arrested for Prohibition violations. Locals, who were children at the time, tell stories about running errands for the detainees, who would slip money to them through the bars. More recently, when the building was renovated, bottles of booze were discovered hidden under the floorboards of some cells.

one body, and a handful of cars that failed to complete the trip down the lake after the harsh, cold, Northern Vermont winter had turned the lake to ice.

During Prohibition people from all over New England used the road that passed both Drown properties on their way to and from "Bush House," a line house located a stone's throw over the border in Quebec. Some people went there to drink, but others went to make money. This latter group, Drown said, loaded their cars full of alcohol, often Molson Blackhorse beer, and brought it back to the States. The bottles were packed in burlap bags full of hay to prevent them from breaking during the ride south. To make their trips more profitable, many smugglers used big, fast cars such as Cadillacs and Packards. And to carry even more booze, some would remove all but the driver's seat.

"Oh, Mother hated those bootleggers," Drown said. Nothing bothered her more than seeing bootleggers speed past the family's house on their way down from Quebec. "Whether they were being chased by the lawmen or not, the smugglers always drove fast," Drown recalled.

From the Bush House, the smugglers' cars charged south across the border along the winding road, first passing the Drown farm,

Lake Memphremagog as seen in a 1907 postcard. The view is looking south from Owl's Head (elevation 2489 ft.) in Quebec. From the middle foreground and beyond is Vermont, with Newport located in the upper right corner. With more than 70 miles of shoreline, this large lake created ample opportunities for smugglers.

and then, a few miles later, taking the hairpin corner in front of the Drown family home. This last turn allowed them to avoid the heart of the city and to connect with one of the area's major roads out of town. "They were heading for places such as Barre, Vermont, and Boston, Massachusetts, where there were lots of thirsty people waiting for the shipments," Drown said. This busy stretch of road was no secret to anyone, he noted, including lawmen.

From the family's farm, he often saw officers on patrol looking for suspicious vehicles. Sometimes they sat in hiding and let bootleggers come to them. Drown witnessed many chases while doing chores, especially while high on the seat of a horse-drawn dump rake that he used to hay the fields around the farm.

Rumrunners had ingenious ways to escape, but probably one of the cleverest was the use of smoke screens to temporarily blind pursuing officers. "Making a smoke screen was easy," Drown said. "The driver, or an accomplice, poured oil through a hole in the car's floor onto the hot muffler below. When the oil hit the muffler it would create a great cloud of blue smoke two hundred feet long."

One day while doing chores, he saw a bootlegger speeding down the road with a lawman tight behind. Suddenly, the driver released a huge smoke screen. The strategy worked. The blinded policeman had to pull over and stop, and the rumrunner kept on going. "It was a great escape for the rumrunner," Drown said.

Bootleggers and lawmen alike had dangerous jobs, he said. Some chases ended with gunfire; others ended in car crashes. Accidents were common on the hairpin turn in front of his parents' house. Speeding cars tried to make the corner too fast and ended up flipping over. Drown remembered one Cadillac in particular; it was piled high with booze and rounding the corner hard when the wooden spokes on the left front wheel suddenly snapped, causing the car to flip over in a loud crash. Its burlap bags full of booze went flying. "There were bottles of Molson all over the road," Drown said. "By the time the police arrived, the neighbors had already carried bags of booze off into the hazelnut bushes, and the bootlegger was long gone."

Another time, a big Studebaker squealed around the corner only to crash several hundred feet up the road. Hearing the crash, Drown and his young friends ran to investigate. "The car and its load had gone into the swamp," he said. "The police were searching with their lights, trying to find the driver. They found his shoes under the pedals of the car, but no bootlegger." Then, a slight

117

movement in a nearby tree caught the children's eyes. "It was the rumrunner, hiding up in a tamarack tree." The policemen didn't ask the children anything, and the children didn't volunteer any information. "They never found him," Drown said with a sly smile.

The following article appeared in the June 11, 1930 issue of the *Orleans County Monitor:*

> An unknown rumrummer attempted to escape with a valuable load of ale by leaving a trail of smoke in the path of the U.S. Patrol Officer following in a Buick Coach. The cars attained a speed of more than a mile a minute at times. The rumrunner made his escape by swimming the Black River after his car had left the highway and sunk beneath the surface of the river.
>
> Immigration patrol officer Earl Meacham, scenting something doing along the border early Wednesday evening, had not long to wait after getting well set on the Lake Road. Following the trail of a Cadillac rum car, he was soon face to face with a dense cloud of smoke that the fleeing car emitted by the use of a smoke-screen attachment. The race, which started not far from the border, continued into Newport City, over Bay, Main, Third, and Pleasant Streets, furnishing considerable excitement to people on the streets.
>
> When well out on the Coventry Road, the oil supply was exhausted, and from then on it was a test of speed between the two cars. The rum car kept well to the left of the highway to prevent the officer passing. The speed of the cars was terrific at times, with the officer overcoming the lead made by the use of the smoke-screen device. In making a right-hand curve on the highway, a mile or more north of Coventry where the Black River runs close to the highway, the rum car took a plunge down a fifteen-foot embankment, settling into the muck bottom in ten feet of water. Officer Meacham, on coming up to the scene, saw the operator in the middle of the stream headed for the opposite shore. He called to him to come back. However, he did not heed the call, but chose to keep on swimming and then to run. Fearing that another might be in the river, the escaping man stopped long enough to assure Meacham that all had escaped.

The car and its cargo of twenty-three cases of 'choice ale' were eventually removed from the car's watery resting place."

The May 13, 1931 issue of the *Monitor* describes a chase in Hyde Park, about forty miles from the border in Lamoille County, that didn't end so happily for the smuggler.

"The seizure of a Cadillac phaeton, 576 bottles of Canadian Ale, 12 bottles of wine, a Chrysler roadster wrecked, and the capture of the driver of the rum car, were the work of U.S. Customs Patrol Officers W. M. Stone and E. E. Revoir patrolling near North Hyde Park early Sunday morning. When they were patrolling in that vicinity at about 6:30 Sunday morning, the Chrysler roadster was seen coming at a fast clip. Having a suspicion that the operator was acting as a rear pilot to a rum car, they took up the chase. They had no trouble in passing the roadster, as en route it was found down over a bank, badly wrecked after turning completely over when it connected with and cut off a telephone pole.

Bent on capturing the rum car, the government car shot through the entanglement of wires placed across the highway when the pole was cut off, overtaking the rumrunner three miles farther south.

The operator of the rum car, leaving his car in gear, stepped to the running board and jumped, hitting the shoestring trail cross-country. The officers shifted their course by plowing through the fence and out across an open field in pursuit of the fleeing man with their automobile, resulting in his capture.

Returning to the highway, they found the Cadillac nearly a quarter of a mile out in a field where it had gone unguided and without damage.

The rum driver was Gerald G. Dudley of North Hyde Park, who was held by U.S. Commissioner Walter H. Cleary under bail of $1,000."

By 1928, the twelve-year-old Jersey had absorbed many of his mother's prohibitionist beliefs. "At that time, I was a staunch prohibitionist." The statute had been waging war against bootleggers since it became law in 1920, and now the young Drown felt it was time to do his part. Picking up his trusty shotgun, Drown walked across the lawn and crouched next to the road, ready for action. He patiently waited for the next outlaw to round the corner. He didn't plan to hurt anybody, he explained; he just wanted to blow out the tires on the next rumrunner's car to come along.

A few minutes later somebody came, all right—his father. Startled at first, his father marched across the lawn, grabbed his son by the back of the neck, and towed him back to the house, all the while telling him he should mind his own business. Drown said he never forgot those words. "I realized that minding my own business was a far smarter thing to do than to try to mind somebody else's," said Drown with a smile as he recalled the scene. "I also gave up being an undercover prohibitionist."

Within a few more years, Drown's temperance sentiments had swung far enough in the other direction that he and a friend decided to try a little bootlegging of their own. The two of them slowly rowed a leaky rowboat six miles up Lake Memphremagog to a Quebec line house. There, the boys purchased two bottles of booze with the money that a Newport storekeeper had given them, and then they achingly rowed the heavy boat back to Newport, scared the entire way.

For their day's labor, the storekeeper gave each boy a hot dog and a soda—hardly adequate pay for the nerve-wracking trip they'd just taken. Drown said he never attempted that gambit again. While getting caught by the lawmen was a deterrent, what really stopped him from continuing his stint as an outlaw was his fear of being caught by his fiery mother. Drown retired from rumrunning, feeling it would be wiser to watch the action from the sidelines.

While Drown may have given up being an outlaw, he never lost his youthful love of adventure and sense of humor. As a seventy-year-old, he was working one day in a wood lot when a hunter mistakenly shot the old forester. The hunter realized his error and ran to Drown's side.

Drown looked up at the hunter and said, "Why did you shoot me?"

The hunter replied, "When I pulled the trigger, I thought you were a bear."

Drown answered, "I know I might not be very good-looking, but I think I'm better-looking than an old bear."

CHAPTER 12

Barbara Grush & Arlene Barnes
"E. B. Webb, Customs Hero"

Barbara Grush of South Hadley, Massachusetts, and her sister, Arlene Barnes of Alexandria, Virginia, have visited the Law Enforcement Memorial in Washington DC, numerous times. The monument commemorates all of the American lawmen that have died in the line of duty. One name on the wall is special to them: U.S. Customs Officer Captain Edward Billings Webb, their father.

A rumrunner shot Captain Webb in the Sunderland Hollow section of Colchester, Vermont, a community on the shores of Lake Champlain, on October 8, 1926. He died several days later of his injuries, at age thirty-five. Webb was stationed in St. Albans, and lived there with his wife, Georgianna, two daughters, and a son.

The death of their father has caused the two women, now in their seventies, to take a much different view of Prohibition than most. While many others may have lost a car or a few bottles of booze because of the law, they lost their father. The sisters spoke of their frustration with the attitude expressed by many during that time.

"Many people simply winked an eye at the lawbreakers and looked the other way," Barnes said. "People didn't consider rumrunning to be breaking the law."

"I think it was a bad law," she continued. "It caused tremendous heartbreak. I think the very worst part of it was that it fostered an acceptance of breaking the law when the law didn't suit you," Barnes said. She believes this attitude remains prevalent to this day. Particularly upsetting to Barnes was how people thought it was fun to outrun the officers. "It may or may not have been a good law, but the officers were only doing their jobs, and in enforcing the law they constantly put their lives on the line. I have no sympathy for lawbreakers," she concluded.

The sisters were very young when their father was killed. Barnes, the younger of the two, has no memories of her father, while the only real memory Grush retains is how each night after work, her father would walk into the house with a surprise for each one of his children stuffed in his pockets.

Then suddenly, their father was gone. "My mother was devastated," Grush said. "She was left with two young daughters and a son. She was so devastated that she never talked about it." She also never remarried, dedicating her life to raising her children. Grush and Barnes said they are proud of their mother for the way she handled such a terrible situation, and credit her with making them the people they are today.

Much of what they know about their father came from other family members, or their father's friends and co-workers who told stories of their father in later years. "They always had such wonderful things to say about him," Barnes said. "I felt I grew to know him from what people said about him." The sisters also cherish the newspaper clippings their mother saved about their father's exploits, including those describing his death.

Captain Webb's death was front-page news in Vermont, covered extensively by many of the state's newspapers. Reporters closely followed the investigation, including the statewide manhunt by lawmen of many agencies. The following article appeared in the October 8, 1926 issue of the *Burlington Free Press*.

> Captain E. B. Webb and Murray Tucker, Customs officers from St. Albans were shot by a man thought to be a rum-runner in Sunderland Hollow about 12:30 this morning. Webb, it is feared is fatally wounded, as a bullet entering his hip passed through the abdomen. Tucker was shot through the wrist. Both men are now in the Mary Fletcher Hospital.
>
> The officers, on watch for a rum-running car, halted a big touring automobile and told the driver they wanted to search it. The driver, who had stopped without question, apparently made no objection, but when Webb was exam-

ining the bottom of the car, the driver pulled a gun and shot the officer in the side of the body. Tucker crashed his flashlight down on the fellow's head, but the blow was not damaging, for the man with the gun fired again and sent a bullet through Tucker's forearm. Then he jumped out of the car, apparently intending to escape. Webb went after him, but the man did some clever ducking, got into the car again, and drove off.

A subsequent manhunt led to the arrest of a New York hotel owner by the name of Walter G. Mason, who, according to a newspaper account, admitted to the crime after his partner, who was not charged in the killing, admitted under grilling by police that Mason had shot the officer. One man was driving a Nash car, the other riding a motorcycle. Mason's confession was recorded in the October 11, 1926 issue of the *Free Press*.

Mason, in telling why he shot Webb, said his purpose was merely to escape. He said he started to get away when the officers opened his door, but Webb held him. There was a struggle in the midst of which Tucker hit him over the head with a flashlight, he said. That crazed him, he claimed, and he fired at Tucker, then turned his gun on Webb."

"The shooting was my mother's worst nightmare come true," Grush said. "She knew my father loved his job, but she worried about him every time he left the door, fearing that something terrible might happen to him. Mother never wanted my father's killer to get out of jail; that's how bitter she was," Grush said. Many years after the shooting, Mason was freed. To prevent their mother from knowing about the release, Grush said, her brother hid all newspaper accounts from her.

It has been several years since the sisters have visited the scene of their father's death, an ordinary stretch of Vermont back road to everyone else. "When I travel down on the Hollow road, I can't do so without thinking about my father and how he died. It gives me an eerie feeling to know that's where he was killed," Grush said.

In happy contrast, the sisters have heard many comforting stories about their father. They find particular solace in an account of the time their father passed up a $15,000 bribe to allow train cars loaded with booze to cross the border for one month. His refusal to succumb to this bribery testifies to their father's honesty and integrity. "He must have been a fine man indeed," said Grush. In an era when many people worked for less than a dollar a day, this was a small fortune (approximately $150,000 in current money).

The April 5, 1921 front-page headline of the *St. Albans Daily Messenger* said it all: Local Customs Officials Trap Man Who Offered $15,000 A Month Bribe. The article details the smuggler's plot that eventually ended in his arrest. Webb's job at the time was inspecting railroad cars for illegal contraband as they entered the country from Canada. Webb was approached by a smuggler from Montreal, Quebec, who wanted to secure the passage of fifteen railroad cars of booze across the border during a one-month period. Each car would contain two hundred cases of alcohol. The smuggler had $2,400 invested in each load, but knew that if he could get this shipment safely into the United States, he could multiply his profits several times over, even with the pay-off to Captain Webb.

Webb's role in the seamy plot was temptingly easy: Informed about the shipments ahead of time, Webb would simply ignore them and let them pass through, receiving $1,000 for every load. Stalling for time, Webb said he was willing but would have to work out a few details before he could accept the first shipment. The smugglers bought the excuse, giving Webb the opportunity to notify his supervisors of the scheme and to set up a trap.

Webb and another officer then met with the smuggler, under the guise of ironing out the details of the scheme. Instead, after the deal making was complete and sufficient evidence gathered, they arrested the smuggler.

Despite the passage of nearly eight decades, the sisters said their father continues to have a profound effect on them. On the dark side was the sadness of not having a father who came home to them every night, as did most of their school friends. On the positive side, they cherish the memories of the good examples they had while growing up—the fine example their father set while on earth and the memories he left behind, and their mother's perseverance and dedication to raising them alone after his death.

"Was it fate or choice?" Barnes wonders, as she reflects on her choice of a husband later in life. "He spent his entire career as an attorney in the United States Department of Justice, prosecuting criminals, including a number of organized crime figures." Either way, an honorable family tradition lives on.

CHAPTER 13

Viola Twiss
"Prohibition: An Idea
Whose Time Has Come?"

Viola Twiss of Windsor, Vermont, has very definite views on alcohol: She condemns people who abuse it, and she would applaud the reinstatement of Prohibition. At the same time, the eighty-five-year-old Twiss, a retired nurse with a jolly personality, vividly recalls the frenzy Prohibition caused in her tiny hometown of Albany, Vermont.

"Oh God, Prohibition provided a lot of excitement in this little town, where we'd never had much before," she said. She laughed at the ruckus created by bootlegging.

Although this small town in Orleans County is located about twenty-five miles south of the U.S.–Canadian border, rumrunners continually passed through Albany on their way south from Quebec. Twiss remembers her schoolhouse days at the Brown School, a one-room affair on Albany's main road. While students often got in trouble for popping up to look at a mysterious Cadillac or Packard racing past, the thrill was usually worth the risk to Twiss and her classmates. "When a rumrunner sped by, we schoolchildren would jump right up out of our seats to see the car, especially if we were near the windows."

With a population in 1920 of 920, and 840 now, Albany was and is a small village. During the twenties, it had two stores that sold groceries and nearly everything else families needed. One of the stores, Hackett's, also housed the town clerk's office. Nowadays there is just one grocery store, and many family farms have been replaced with new homes. Both then and now, the town has a confusing network of small, unpaved roads that can easily befuddle visitors.

A couple of miles from the village of Albany on the Shuteville Road, Twiss was born on March 19, 1916, to Joseph and Sula Gonyaw. She was just two years old when her mother died, so has no memory of her. Her father raised Viola and her three brothers and one sister on the family's farm. "My father never remarried because he didn't trust anybody else to raise his children," Twiss said. "He took caring for his children seriously, and he believed in making his money honestly."

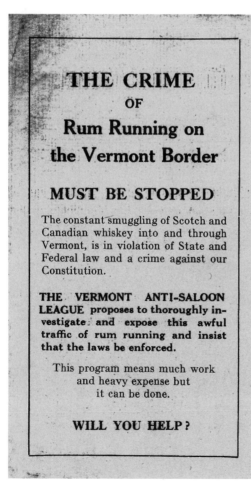

THE CRIME
OF
Rum Running on the Vermont Border

MUST BE STOPPED

The constant smuggling of Scotch and Canadian whiskey into and through Vermont, is in violation of State and Federal law and a crime against our Constitution.

THE VERMONT ANTI-SALOON LEAGUE proposes to thoroughly investigate and expose this awful traffic of rum running and insist that the laws be enforced.

This program means much work and heavy expense but it can be done.

WILL YOU HELP?

This pamphlet was published by the Vermont Chapter of the nationally-based Anti-Saloon League, which was an indefatigable publisher of temperance and Prohibition literature. This piece called on Vermonters to come to the aid of authorities, who were understaffed for the task of stopping rum-running. Arguably, this direct appeal to the citizenry indicates that though Prohibition was the law of the land, citizens did not necessarily feel that they needed to obey the regulation.

Twiss also credited her sister, Blanche, the eldest child in the family, for helping her father raise all of the children with a strong moral code. Twiss noted that Blanche refused to marry until all of her siblings were grown, and she felt she had fulfilled her role as a mother to them.

Life at home was not easy. "It was the Depression, and money was tight," Twiss recalled. "Some people sold alcohol to make extra money, but not my father. He juggled several honest jobs instead: He farmed, he logged, he had a sugar bush, and he sold wild horses from out west. All in all, he worked like the devil," Twiss said. "He was very, very honest, and he taught us to be honest, too."

He also believed in helping folks in time of need, including those who found their cars stuck during the spring thaw mud season, when dirt roads can become nearly impassable. It was common at this time of year for many cars—some loaded with alcohol— to get stuck on her family's road.

Twiss said that many unfortunate souls found their way to the family's door and begged her father to pull them out. It was rela- tively easy to identify the smugglers: They were impatient, anxious to get out before the police or Customs officers spotted their stranded cars. Because Gonyaw didn't own a car, he hitched up his workhorses and walked the team to the mired vehicles. Twiss remembers the first time a rumrunner came looking for help. "Someone walked to our door and said to my father, 'Can you take your workhorses and pull me out of the mud a half mile down the road?' Dad didn't think twice about pulling the fellow's car out; he just did it.

"Later, after getting the car out, he walked back into the farm- house and said to all of us, 'I don't know if I should have done that or not. That car was full of liquor,'" Twiss recalled. The fact that the driver of the Cadillac gave him a twenty-dollar bill helped ease his conscience a bit. "A twenty back then was a lot of money—a couple of weeks' wages for a laborer," Twiss said. "None of us children had ever even seen such a large bill before." Although Gonyaw would accept money, he refused alcohol in exchange for his services. "If they wanted to give him liquor, he'd say no," his daughter said.

Gonyaw wanted nothing to do with one notorious rumrunner who was well known in Vermont, New York, and Canada. Called the One-Handed Outlaw because he was missing a hand and had a hook in its place, it was said that he once used the hook to kill a lawman. The bootlegger and his gray-haired girlfriend showed up at the Gonyaw house one night looking for a place to sleep and hide their Cadillac. "Seeing the hook," Twiss said, "my father knew instantly who the fellow was. Dad said, 'You better step on the gas and get out of my sight, because I've heard about you.' The man took his advice and left.

"Dad thought Prohibition was foolishness," Twiss said. She said her father enjoyed an occasional drink, especially during haying season when one of his sons would brew up a batch of beer. At the same time, he couldn't abide men who neglected or abused their families as a result of their drinking. He belonged to the Orleans County Log Rollers, a civic group of the time and similar to the Elks Club of today, except that some members also acted as unofficial lawmen. Twiss explained how they operated: "The members believed in a man drinking, but not in getting drunk. If someone was drinking and not taking care of his family, and doing things he shouldn't, members would catch the offender, tie him into a chair with his head tipped back, put a gallon of liquor to his mouth, and start pouring. The offender had to swallow. I don't know how much

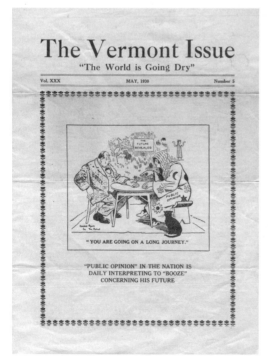

The *Vermont Issue* was published by the local chapter of the Anti-Saloon League, which published the *American Issue*. Note the paper's motto: "The World is Going Dry." Had Twiss been reading pro-temperance literature in 1930, she might have seen this bit of ill-fated prediction: On the cover a palmist interprets the hand of a man representing "Booze" and informs him that he "is going on a long journey." In fact, the tide had already turned on Prohibition and less than three years later it had been repealed.

they poured, but when they got through with him he was either cured and never drank again, or he was dead." Twiss said she doesn't know if her father ever took part in treating anybody with this particular kill-or-cure method.

There's little doubt in Viola Twiss's mind that Prohibition was a good idea. "It's better that liquor not be sold anywhere," she said. "The country would be a better place if the law hadn't been repealed. I think drinking should be handled the way they're dealing with tobacco these days—it should be stopped altogether. It does nothing but harm. Before Prohibition," she noted, "too many people who drank—otherwise decent people,—ended up neglecting or abusing their families." It's her opinion that people were happier during Prohibition because fewer families had to suffer at the hands of drunkards.

"And these days it seems as though people think they have to drink to have a good time," she lamented. To her recollection, that wasn't the case during Prohibition. People loved to dance, especially at kitchen junkets, but there was little, if any, drinking involved. "When I had a junket, we'd move all the furniture out of the big room and we'd dance," she said. "Somebody would play the fiddle." The family also went to the dances at the Grange Hall in town, where somebody played the piano or violin. Twiss remembers dancing on her father's feet when she was two or three years old. "My father would rather dance than eat," she laughed.

When she left the local schoolhouse after eighth grade, Twiss attended Craftsbury Academy. Because the school was too far from home for Twiss to travel back and forth each day, she rented a room in Craftsbury for a dollar a week. "A dollar was a lot of money back then," she said. To help make the weekly payments, she worked summers in Newport. As a thirteen- and fourteen-year-old, she waited tables at the Allen Dale Farm, where many out-of-town visitors stayed in a large guesthouse near the shores of Lake Memphremagog. Twiss earned a dollar a week, enough to pay for her lodging.

The farm also owned seven camps along the lake, Twiss recalled. To make extra money, Twiss occasionally baby-sat for the guests that were staying in the camps. While she had heard rumors about rumrunners using the lake to smuggle booze, she never saw anything until one eventful evening. "I heard a big racket. There was a powerboat loaded with liquor coming down

Skinner's Cave, also known as Smuggler's Cave, on Lake Memphremagog. This cave has served smugglers for hundreds of years.

the lake, and close behind were police in a second boat, shooting at the first boat. One of the bullets came into the camp where I was babysitting and hit the wall." When she told her father about the episode, he made her come home to Albany. The next summer, Twiss was allowed to work again at the farm, but not to take any babysitting jobs down at the camps.

During the school year, talk of rumrunners and alcohol was taboo. "Life at the academy was strict," Twiss said, "so strict that you wouldn't have dared to say 'liquor.' Many people believed no self-respecting young girl would even talk about such topics," Twiss said.

"Even so," Twiss said, "like young people today, some back then went to Canada to drink." She remembered one trip ending in a car crash that killed a young Craftsbury boy. "In a small town, that was a very sorrowful thing," she recalled.

"While Prohibition cut down on the amount of drinking, it certainly didn't stop it," Twiss admitted. People could either go to Canada to drink, buy it from somebody who sold it, or make their own. A lot of people had stills, making alcohol for their own use or for resale. Twiss told the story of one neighbor who kept three stills on his property. "That was the way he made his living. To fool the lawmen that often raided his operation, the fellow would use only one of the stills, which was well hidden, and keep the two unused stills where they could easily be found. The lawmen would come, kick over the two stills, then leave thinking they'd accomplished their job. My neighbor was left chuckling."

Twiss remembers Prohibition being repealed in 1933, but she recalls no fanfare about the decision. She does remember that life calmed down, though, as rumrunners and revenuers—but not alcohol—dried up in her part of the Kingdom.

CHAPTER 14

William "Dig" Rowley
"Everything Was Against Them"

Lawmen probably caught only about 10 percent of the bootleggers in Vermont during Prohibition. The remaining 90 percent either managed to cross the border with their illicit cargo unnoticed, or managed to outwit or outrun officers who attempted to cut short their trips to the south. Those aren't official government statistics, but the observations of retired U.S. Customs officer William "Dig" Rowley, age ninety, of Richford, Vermont.

"Everything was against them," Rowley said of the lawmen's plight. "It was difficult to demand compliance with a law that so many Americans disliked, and few provisions were made to help the Customs and Immigration officers whose duty it was to guard the border and to enforce federal laws, including Prohibition.

"Prohibition was simply an unenforceable law, and many Americans, including Vermonters, took advantage of that," Rowley said. Both public attitudes and a lack of equipment made the work more difficult. Officers often had to rely on vehicles seized from smugglers to chase down other smugglers. They also didn't have the communications equipment that we take for granted today. Without two-way radios, officers could not effectively coordinate the pursuit and capture of bootleggers after they had sped across the border.

Rowley is a stout, balding, handsome man with a sharp memory, crisp voice, and a quick wit. He was born in Richford, a tiny industrial railroad town on the western flank of the Green

Mountains in the Missisquoi River basin of Franklin County. Rowley lives not far from the center of town in the house he and his late wife, Marion, shared for many years. Dozens of old pictures hang on the walls, and hundreds more fill boxes throughout the house. His love for, and knowledge of, his community has earned him the respect of all, both in town and in Montpelier. In 1993, the Vermont Legislature proclaimed Rowley the "Official Unofficial Mayor of Richford."

Long before his honorary mayoralty, though, Rowley was just a young man growing up in Richford during Prohibition, and he saw plenty of bootlegging action in his border community. In 1945, twelve years after Prohibition was repealed, he joined the U.S. Customs Service and had the opportunity to work with Customs officers who had been charged with enforcing Prohibition. From them he heard many stories about their ill-fated campaigns to stop the flow of illegal alcohol coming into America from Canada. Guarding the border, located just two miles north of town, was a daunting task.

The bootleggers were highly motivated by the potential reward of good money to be made. They were equally determined to avoid capture and possible hard time in prison. "Those bootleggers were some smart," Rowley said. "They were always thinking of better ways to escape the lawmen that patrolled the border communities." One favorite contrivance used to help escape pursuing lawmen was the smoke screen generator, which left a billowing cloud of black smoke in the wake of the speeding rumrunner's car. The

Main Street, Richford, Vermont, circa 1920.

road would become so obscured that the frustrated lawmen would have to pull over, giving up the chase.

Some rumrunners made a smoke screen by simply pouring oil through a hole in the floor onto the hot muffler below. More sophisticated operators had a switch on the dashboard that opened and closed a canister under the car's hood. When the driver threw the switch, the container opened and dumped a mixture of oil and ammonia onto the hot manifold below. "The ammonia would smart your eyes, and the old oil would make a filthy dark cloud," said Rowley.

Rowley laughed about the time he saw a smoke screen from a smuggler's point of view. In 1929, he and a friend were hitchhiking back to Richford when a black Cadillac pulled up alongside them. The driver said gruffly, "If you want a ride, get in. You'll have to pull the jump seat open.

"Oh, he was a tough-looking little fellow, with his derby hat cocked to one side." When the two young men climbed in, they realized immediately that the fellow was a bootlegger on his way home from a booze run. The car's backseat had been removed to make room for more bottles of liquor. The only things back there were beer and liquor wrappers scattered about the floor. No sooner had their ride begun than things started getting lively.

"We were going like hell for those days," Rowley said. "We went around a corner, and there were some young cattle in the road. All of them got out of the road except for this young bull. Well, we hit the bull and knocked it end over end, but the driver kept on go-

This 1927 photograph of the U.S. Border Patrol, Newport service, shows an impressive group of 13 agents. This number pales, though, when compared to the vast territory—roughly 4,200 square miles— under their jurisdiction.

ing. The collision had jarred the car something fierce, and all of the sudden, thick black smoke began to roll out of the old car. We were in the backseat, so it didn't affect us. Looking over our shoulders, out the back window, you couldn't see a thing. Meanwhile, the driver was frantically fiddling with a switch on the dashboard as we careened along. We just hoped he was paying enough attention to stay on the road. And then suddenly, the smoke stopped."

Bootleggers relied on the good will of those living along their route. "Many people were against Prohibition, and Richford was no exception," Rowley said. People living along busy smuggling routes had a pretty good idea of when officers were patrolling, and they were willing to share that information with smugglers. Some farmers let bootleggers use their barns to hide their cars, especially during a chase to avoid capture. The cars pulled into the barns, and if the officers didn't see them go in, they drove by thinking they were still in pursuit.

"Cows were part of another common escape strategy. They were used as roadblocks to delay the lawmen," Rowley said. Some farmers who didn't get directly involved in the alcohol business did conspire with their bootlegger friends. They scheduled it so the cows would cross the road from one pasture to another at about the same time the friend was passing by with a load. As soon as the bootlegger passed, the farmer would quickly lead the cows into the road just in case an officer was in pursuit. A bunch of cows standing in the middle of the road was an effective roadblock for impatient officers, who fell victim to the ploy. The officer, bootlegger, and farmer all knew the likelihood of capture decreased with every second the officer had to wait.

"Not everybody in Richford was against Prohibition," Rowley said. "My mother was all for it. While my father didn't care, my mother was deathly against alcohol." The town had an active and vocal chapter of the Women's Christian Temperance Union (WCTU), a national organization that wanted nothing less than the complete elimination of alcohol. Such supporters of Prohibition were more than happy to tip off lawmen to the smuggling activities along their roads.

"Collaborating with the cops had its risks however," Rowley said. "Some bootleggers weren't afraid to use intimidation to silence tipsters. One family in town got a package one day, and it contained a miniature coffin—as much as to say, 'Maybe you're going to be needing one of these if you continue.'" According to Rowley, the message worked, and the tips to the police stopped.

Richford's location on the border with Canada made it a major player in the highly lucrative bootlegging scene. The town offered a maze of backcountry roads and unguarded border crossings. Soon the town was on one of the busiest and most direct routes from the Montreal distilleries and breweries to New York City, the thirstiest metropolis in the country. The traffic was heavy, and no other smuggling endeavor was as profitable: A case of the best Canadian whiskey purchased in Montreal for ten dollars brought eighty dollars from New York buyers.

The smuggling business attracted people from all walks of life. "It's easy to understand why people got involved in bootlegging," Rowley said. "Money was tight, especially during the Depression years—and bootlegging was very profitable." Many smugglers were loners, but some operators joined forces to create powerful Vermont syndicates.

One Vermont syndicate was headquartered in Barre, the first destination of many carloads of alcohol. One Barre syndicate set up a repair garage in Richford, ostensibly to offer its services to the public. In reality, the garage was a front. The shop's real purpose was to keep the syndicate's fleet of cars in top condition for their runs from Montreal to Barre, and then on to destinations in southern New England, where it seemed the demand for good Canadian whiskey was insatiable.

"A lot of the young guys did some rum-running just for the hell of it," Rowley said. "These thrill-seekers were the 'small fry.' A fair number of local men would sneak a few bottles home from a night in Canada," he said. Getting a little liquor over the border was not too difficult given that the customshouse was located in town, not at the border itself. The small fry could simply take a side street and bypass Customs entirely.

"The officers didn't generally bother with the locals," Rowley said. "They were more interested in catching the big boys with the big loads than chasing down a person who slipped across with a bottle or two of booze." Rowley noted, however, that some local men weren't satisfied with just a bottle or two; they liked the thrill of bringing a larger load across. They'd bring alcohol home by the case—sometimes loaded in a car, other times in a small boat on the Missisquoi River that flows south from Quebec and passes

The Missisquoi River as it flows over the dam and through Richford, circa 1910. Presumably even the most inebriated smuggler pulled ashore before the dam.

through town. Most of these smugglers drank it themselves, but some sold it to friends, usually making only fifty cents or so on a bottle—much less than the pros.

"The big bootleggers from outside of the area took their jobs more seriously," Rowley said. "They did it for the profits, and they had invested a lot money in their operations. Some were wild characters prone to violence, something more than one law-man found out." The September 7, 1927 issue of the *Orleans County Monitor* describes the close call that a pair of lawmen had with a couple of gun-toting outlaws:

United States Immigration Patrol Officers Benner and Standish, of the Richford office, had a narrow escape from serious injury or even death early Wednesday morning when the occupants of a touring car, which they were pursuing, fired at them with a revolver. One of the shots went through the windshield of the officers' car, while the other hit the radiator.

They saw an automobile of the open touring type, approaching them at a fast clip. A car traveling at this fast rate of speed at this time of the morning naturally made the government men suspicious. At any rate, they figured—and naturally, too—that they had a perfect right to stop the machine and see if it was loaded with either liquor or human contraband. They gave the usual signal to stop, but the driver ignored the warning and stepped on the gas. The machine sped past the officers like an arrow from a bow. The patrolmen then hopped into their Ford and took after the speeding machine.

It was at this time that the occupants of the suspected car started to re-enact a battle scene. One man apparently opened fire with a revolver. His aim was good, for a bullet came crashing through the Ford's windshield, missing the two officers by only a fraction of an inch. A second shot hit the radiator. Then the Ford stopped. That the man behind the gun was not fooling is perfectly evident. From where the bullets lodged it would appear that the marksman was shooting straight, and shooting to kill rather than to maim.

Captain Ernest R. Harvey, Customs patrol leader, was advised of the shooting by the Immigration men. Harvey immediately ordered two of his patrol cars to take the road in the search for the suspected liquor or human bootleggers who did the firing.

The Customs patrolmen combed this entire section during the night without any favorable results. They combed all the main highways and many of the back roads, but could find no trace of the machine that was described to Captain Harvey as the one the men who fired at the Immigration men were riding in.

One suggestion advanced was that the men who did the shooting might have turned their car around and headed back into Canada after doing the firing, reasoning that the Immigration men would have notified fellow officers south of Richford who would be on the watch for them.

The search has not been given up as yet, however, as the registration number of the suspected machine is known to the Immigration and Customs patrolmen who are keeping close watch on the roads for the car and its passengers.

Rowley also had a friend who learned the hard way that smugglers couldn't be trusted. Rowley's friend sold large quantities of alcohol from his barn in town. There were always a half-dozen or so big cars there, loading up with booze. Gunfire erupted one day when a smuggler apparently didn't want to pay his bill. "The rumrunner started to pay him," Rowley said, "but instead of taking out the money, he took out a revolver and shot my friend in the hand." The outlaw fled in the loaded car, but was eventually apprehended by the police.

It wasn't difficult to tell when a big-time smuggler in town, Rowley said. "If you saw a Pierce Arrow, a Cadillac, a big old

Packard, or any car like that, it was one of two things: a million-aire or a bootlegger." Most people in town were too poor to afford even a small, cheap car, to say nothing of those big, expensive cars that could carry payloads of up to a ton, or between three and five hundred quart bottles. The bottles weighed three or more pounds each and were stuffed a dozen at a time in burlap bags.

The locals who could afford cars usually had Model T Fords, or later, Model A Fords, because they were smaller and cheaper. If used for smuggling, the Fords could hold only a fraction of the booze the big cars could haul. "More than one of those cheap little cars were dumped in this area because the local boys, seeing they were about to be stopped, jumped out and let the car go," Rowley said. "They didn't have much money invested in it. Many ended up in the river."

For those with a thirst for alcohol but no stomach for smuggling, the bars and hotels of Abercorn, Quebec, were close at hand. Because few people had cars, there was a ready clientele for the taxis that regularly queued up in Richford. For twenty-five cents, taxi drivers would take their customers across the border for an evening of drinking. The hotels had colorful names, such as the Abercorn House, Prince Albert Inn, and Prince of Wales. "They were places where you could go dance and buy your beer." Many of the younger people who crossed the border weren't experi-enced at drinking, so things could get a little wild, Rowley said. "There would be a lot of scraps."

Although drinking was legal in Quebec, the hotels did have rules to follow. One rule said that when alcohol was sold, it must be served with food. Rowley laughed as he described the ruse em-ployed by many bars: The Famous Cheese Sandwich. "When you had a beer, they'd bring you a plate with a sandwich and set it down beside you. That sandwich would be so old that the corners would be turned right up. Nobody ever ate it. No one would ever have dreamed of eating it. When you were done drinking, the plate was taken away and the sandwich was saved for the next fellow," Rowley chuckled.

Beyond the regular bars and hotels, there were other unique spots that offered alcohol and diversion. "One such place," said Rowley, "was a little shack with a colorful name—The Bucket of Blood." Rowley doesn't know how the place got its name, and he never went there because the younger generation wasn't welcome.

There was a farmer just across the border who sold alcohol from his kitchen. With a wink, Rowley said he visited the place more than once.

People involved in the illegal alcohol trade were typically men, but that's not to say there weren't a handful of women involved as well. A number of women, most of them homegrown Vermonters, made big names for themselves during Prohibition. Perhaps the most famous of them all was Richford resident Lillian Fleury, better known as Queen Lil. Queen Lil owned and operated a bar and brothel built smack-dab on the international border in East Richford.

Queen Lil was more than a pretty face; she was a shrewd businesswoman who understood the importance of knowing the right people and supporting the right causes. She supported Prohibition as well as the local WCTU, not because she wanted an end to alcohol, but because she saw that the law created customers for her own bar business.

Gregarious and likeable, Queen Lil, even with the shady side of her reputation, endeared herself to many people in the Richford area. And from her early days in Boston, she maintained connections far outside of Vermont. These associations helped her remain out of the clutches of the lawmen—most of the time.

One of her favorite tactics was moving contraband from one side of the border to the other, all within her establishment. When she'd hear that a raid by American lawmen was imminent, she moved her cache of booze to the Canadian side of the house. When the officers came knocking, there was little they could do, even though they knew there was alcohol only a few feet away. They had no jurisdiction in Canada—even when Canada was in the same house.

Queen Lil's connections reached into the Canadian side as well. Whenever Canadian officers raided her business in an attempt to close her down for a variety of reasons, they'd always find that she had already moved the business to the American side of the house.

Frustrated by her brazenness, American and Canadian lawmen joined forces at least once to stage a joint raid. They did manage, finally, to bring charges, but not to put her out of business. Not until Lil herself chose to retire did her house close its doors permanently. Some people reveled in her retirement, while more than a few men were despondent.

"People from all over New England passed through Richford on their journey across the border to drink," Rowley said. "Some came by car, but many came by train." He recalled the "Beer Special Trains" that passed through Richford on the way to Montreal, Quebec. The trains originated in Lowell, Massachusetts, and picked up people along the way. "They wanted to go where they could cut loose and have a hell of a time. They wanted to whoop it up. They wanted their beer, they wanted their alcohol, so they would take an excursion to Canada where they could get it by the trainload." As the weekend came to a close, the train headed south, hauling the exhausted revelers home. "Some of them were sicker than hell," Rowley recollected.

When Canadian passenger trains crossed the border into Richford, Customs officers boarded them in search of people trying to smuggle a bottle or two of alcohol back into the States. So began a cat-and-mouse game that the Customs agents knew well. The passengers hid the bottles; those sitting on the side of the train away from the station often dangled bottles out of the windows on strings to avoid having them confiscated. Customs agents had seen just about every trick there was, however, so an officer would routinely walk along the backside of the train cutting the strings and collecting bottles as he went.

"It was the freight trains from Quebec that gave Customs officers their biggest challenge," Rowley said. "While they might find

The Richford railroad station, built in 1906, and shown above circa 1915. Richford was a busy railroad center and was served by two different railroads. The town was connected with St. Albans, 27 miles to the west, and Newport, 21 miles to the east.

a few bottles of alcohol on a passenger train, on the freight trains there could be hundreds, sometimes thousands, of bottles—or even barrels—of booze buried in cargo that ran the gamut from apples to hay, lumber to zucchini." Finding the booze was exhausting, as it often meant unloading half the contents of the cars.

Seized alcohol was later smashed, Rowley said. He recalled watching Customs officers breaking heavy, green bottles on a rocky ledge along the river. The bottles were so strong that it took a powerful blow to break them. "Some of those bottles, unless you hit them just right, wouldn't break, and they'd skid into the river. The kids used to swim down there and pick up the ones that got away from the agents."

Even far from the border, Rowley said that alcohol was readily available during Prohibition. Traveling to Albany, New York, with a friend, he visited a speakeasy—an illegal drinking establishment. Rowley's friend had been there many times before, and he vouched for Rowley. "People couldn't just walk in. You rapped on a locked, windowless door, and the attendant on the inside would pull a little bar open and look out to see who you were. If they knew you, or you came with someone they trusted, they'd let you in."

Customers didn't generally have much of a selection of drinks to choose from, Rowley said. "In those days they didn't have so many fancy drinks. A lot of people drank their liquor straight.

"They were getting two dollars and a quarter for a bottle of beer in Albany," Rowley said. "Well, a rumrunner was probably paying twenty cents for that bottle of beer up here, so you can see the profit to be made; even if they lost a car once in a while, they could still make money.

"Unfortunately, Prohibition brought its share of pain," Rowley said. At least one Customs officer was killed in Vermont by a smuggler, and many people were injured or killed in car crashes. Others died or suffered permanent side effects from drinking bad alcohol. People who couldn't get their hands on liquor or beer turned to more questionable substances. Vanilla, used for cooking, and many patent medicines and tonics contained a large percentage of alcohol and had little ill effect. But people also drank wood alcohol, rubbing alcohol, and "Sterno," used in heaters—all of which could kill or cripple. A common detoxification method involved straining the liquids through a loaf of bread. People mistakenly believed that this process would filter out the poisonous chemicals and other impurities.

141

"What dripped out of the loaf was supposed to be good alcohol, which it wasn't," Rowley said. "It was a damn wonder that everybody who drank it didn't die." Rowley knew of one person who went blind and another who lost the use of his legs from drinking bad alcohol.

Rowley said that when he joined Customs in 1945, he had the opportunity to work with some of the Customs officers who had enforced Prohibition. He enjoyed listening to their stories about the many bootleggers they had encountered—both the small fry and the big fry—including the ones that got away. The agents said that stopping the flow of booze into America was impossible. "Most of the officers were honorable men who believed in enforcing the law," Rowley said, "but that didn't mean they liked the law or believed in it. Regardless, hired to enforce the statute, they tried their best, even when that enforcement was unpopular."

CHAPTER 15

Anatole Duquette
"Moonshine and the Morning Glass"

"Ten pounds of corn, ten pounds of sugar, and ten pounds of yeast, all placed in a ten-gallon milk can partially filled with water. That's about all it took to get the mash going," said Anatole Duquette of Barton, Vermont, as he recalled the first step in his family's moonshining. "Sometimes my mother would throw a few prunes into the mixture, perhaps for a little extra flavor.

"It was simple," Duquette said. "Anybody could make a batch of moonshine, and many people did." Duquette, now in his early nineties, said that making their own liquor was just part of keeping a family tradition alive. "We were just providing my father with his morning glass of whiskey. This was a ritual he began back in Quebec long before Prohibition. It was also part of the culture; many other French-Canadian immigrants had the same way of starting the day.

"We never really thought of moonshining as breaking the law; no, we were law-abiding folks . . . and still are. In fact, my brother's boy, J. Paul Duquette, is the chief of police in Newport, Vermont," Duquette proudly pointed out. The family didn't abuse the alcohol they made, and only family and visiting relatives from Quebec drank it, Duquette explained. His father refused to sell their moonshine, even though his immigrant family could have used the money as they tried to sweat out a living as farmers. Duquette's father also refused to allow smugglers to hide their rum-running vehicles in his barn, as so many other farmers would do for a price. "Dad was an honest man, a man of ethics," Duquette said. "There was no price high enough to get him to sell out his moral principles."

Anatole Duquette was born on June 1, 1911, in Laprie, Quebec. He immigrated with his parents, Auguste and Virginia Duquette, when he was a young boy, and they settled just twenty miles south of the U.S.–Canadian border in Barton, Vermont, a farming community in Orleans County. They moved into a rambling old fourteen-room farmhouse and did their best to make a living, working long hours each day on their dairy farm.

Life was difficult, and little changed for Duquette over the years. Although he did not completely shun the conveniences of the modern world, the old bachelor has never owned a car or gotten his driver's license. Never married, he dedicated his life to caring for his parents, who both lived well into old age.

Worn by weather and years of labor, the old farmer only recently sold his cows and the family's homestead that he called home most of his life. Duquette moved into the village and bought a trailer, where he surrounds himself with memorabilia of his younger years. In a thick French-Canadian accent, Duquette reminisces about the old days, fondly recalling his youth and memories of his parents.

BARTON, VT. HOTEL BARTON.

The Barton House, Barton, Vermont, circa 1910. Country inns such as this one suffered when Prohibition came into effect, as clients who wished to drink were drawn to Quebec, which lay only twenty miles to the north.

"There were few folks then who *didn't* have a batch of moonshine around the house," Duquette said warmly. "Some drank the brew to get drunk, others to relax, and some, like my father, as a ritual. Others called their moonshine 'medicine' and drank it when something ailed them." Duquette doesn't know if the moonshine ever did cure any ills, but he has little doubt that those suffering from various ailments, real or imaginary, gained some relief by drinking alcohol, especially when consumed in large doses.

"Many folks made their own moonshine, and there wasn't just one way to make it," Duquette continued. "People had different recipes, and they brewed and distilled in all sorts of homemade contraptions." Some had elaborate stills that were capable of producing large amounts of moonshine. Others made it as his family did—in milk cans—the cans that farmers normally used to carry their milk to the creamery.

In the Duquette household, the concoction was mixed together in the kitchen and then the can was lugged upstairs to Anatole's bedroom, where it sat for about four days to soak. "My job was to shake it up every night to keep the mash from compacting on the bottom, which prevented it from fermenting completely. The better the brew fermented, the stronger the final product," Duquette said. "We used my bedroom because a stovepipe passed through it. We'd set the can next to the pipe to keep the mash warm and help it ferment into alcohol. You had to keep that stuff hot," he pointed out, "and that wasn't an easy task during the winter months." Drafty Vermont farmhouses such as Duquette's had little, if any, insulation to help keep the winter cold out.

Once the mash had finished fermenting, the can was hauled back down to the kitchen. The contents were then poured through a strainer, which caught the mash solids while the liquid passed into a large kettle below. The kettle was put on the stove for distilling. Wasting nothing, the family fed the strainerful of mash to their poultry. Duquette muses on this, wondering with a chuckle if perhaps the flock didn't get a bit tipsy on the alcohol-soaked mixture.

All these years later, Duquette has a difficult time explaining the strange-looking homemade apparatus used to distill the moonshine. He explained that the liquid was brought to a boil in the kettle, and the rising vapors were captured and condensed back to a liquid, which was then collected in a second kettle. The contents of this second kettle were finished moonshine. "Sometimes, though, my father wanted a stronger batch, and in that case, the moonshine was distilled again. This time the end result was one hundred-percent alcohol—that's two hundred-proof moonshine!" said Duquette, almost shuddering at the thought. "Depending on how strong we were making the moonshine, we'd get between one and three gallons from each batch."

"My father was very moderate with his alcohol. I can only recall one time when I saw my father tipsy, and that was after he'd sampled too much of a friend's moonshine," Duquette recalled. As a regular participant in his family's whiskey-making, and being a teenager at the time, Duquette admitted that he was curious about alcohol. He occasionally sampled the moonshine, but, like his father, he didn't believe in overindulgence. It wasn't until after Prohibition ended that he got drunk for his first and last time. He started out by just having one drink, but by the time he was done, he'd consumed a large quantity of two different kinds of booze. Duquette couldn't walk without the assistance of two friends. "That is the only time I ever got drunk, and I learned something from it," he said with a wise smile.

"Everybody always claimed that they made the best moonshine, and it seemed everybody was always trying to make it a little better," remembered Duquette. For those looking mainly to get drunk, "best" just meant higher proof. For others, creating a good-tasting liquor was the goal. "Most folks had very simple stills," said Duquette, "but serious producers, people interested in making enough to sell, had larger and more elaborate set-ups.

"While many folks made moonshine, you didn't talk about it. People who bragged about their moonshining operations were typically all mouth, or weren't long for the business," said Duquette. "Although most people around town minded their own business, there was always a handful of temperance-minded folk who were more than happy to volunteer whatever they heard about brewing or distilling to local, state, and federal lawmen.

"People making a few bottles or so for family use weren't a high priority for the lawmen," Duquette said. "They were more interested in finding the renegade moonshiners who shunned the law and supplied the county with high-proof alcohol—stuff many times stronger than any beer that was crossing the border." Desperate to avoid detection, these big-time still operators used a host of tricks to hide their work. Springtime sugaring operations were often just fronts for their distilling. Other moonshiners took to the deep woods with their homemade stills to avoid detection. "Some illegal distillers hid elaborate brewing operations deep in caves," said Duquette, "but even these well-hidden spots were discovered by the lawmen, especially when the serious federal boys, the revenuers, participated in the hunt."

Despite the modest size of his family's operation, Duquette said that his father always feared being raided by police officers. "They were searching everybody if they thought you were making liquor. If they heard rumors that moonshine was being made at a certain house, the officers raided it and searched the property. Oh, they looked everywhere imaginable. Sometimes they came up empty-handed. Other times they managed to shut a still down—at least temporarily."

The November 10, 1920 issue of the *Orleans County Monitor* reported on still-busting operations:

> "Information has recently been coming to State's Attorney Frank D. Thompson that moonshiners were operating in the hills and mountains of Albany and Lowell, and that many stills were making moonshine whiskey.
> These reports became so numerous that the state's attorney started a quiet investigation that has been going on for some weeks. He called to his assistance James R. Wood, of the James R. Wood Detective Agency of Boston, aid of Deputy Sheriff George E. Jennings and G. A. Humphrey; the woods around Barton and Albany were combed. As a result of their night labors, four illicit stills have been raided, a considerable quantity of home brew was seized, and four men were arrested."

"My family's house was never raided," said Duquette, "but the stress of worrying about a raid convinced my father to quit moonshining. He carefully rationed his remaining bottles of homemade whiskey."

While the Duquette's moonshining operation was harmless, not everyone who moonshined was as peaceable as his family. People living in Barton were surprised when, on May 16, 1930, a decomposing body was found on the shores of Crystal Lake, a beautiful, clear lake just south of the village.

The May 21, 1930 issue of the *Orleans County Monitor* reported the discovery:

"The body of a man later identified by the clothing as that of Grover Hemmings of Mount Airy, North Carolina, and Beebe, Quebec, was discovered by Fred Martell, Jr., Friday afternoon as he was trolling for fish in Crystal Lake, two and a half miles south of Barton village. He was a few rods out in the lake not far from the Fred Hemmings place when he saw this strange object upon the beach, hidden from the highway not far distant by a low bank. Rowing nearer, Mr. Martelle saw that it was the body of a man and immediately went ashore to notify authorities."

Five days later, in the May 21, 1930 issue of the *Orleans County Monitor*, the story behind the mysterious body's appearance had been worked out by investigators:

"Mr. Hemmings has been employed in Beebe for some months as a stonecutter, but was apparently employed in smuggling on the side—for on the night of November 29, he and an unidentified companion were driving a liquor-laden car and given chase by officers from a point in Derby to a point out of Barton village, where the liquor car was ditched. In the dark, one man ran east toward Crystal Lake, only a few rods away, while the second party ran west to the woods above and across the railroad track. Officers followed some tracks both ways for a short distance, but saw there was no use following in the dark. A little later they thought they heard a cry for help from the lake and went to investigate, but seeing no signs of distress and hearing no further cries, believed the cry might be a ruse to get them from the car.

The next day State's Attorney Miles and Sheriff Gray visited the spot upon the request of the Customs officials, but inquiry of those living nearby and examination of the field, shore, and ice gave no clues to suspect the grim tragedy that apparently took place in the icy water of Crystal Lake the evening before."

This set of pictures shows confiscated distilling apparatus. The equipment above is used in the first half of the moonshining process; the equipment below is used in the second half.

The picture above shows a large operation's "mash tun," the vessel in which grains are cooked in order to convert their sugars into a form more readily fermented by yeast into alcohol. Fermentation can only yield about 10–14 percent alcohol, at which point the alcohol becomes toxic to the yeast, killing it and ending alcohol production. To create liquor—moonshine—the alcohol must be separated out and concentrated. This is achieved by distilling—heating the mixture to vaporize the more volatile alcoholic portion of the mixture, which is then recaptured through condensation.

The equipment below consists mainly of distilling apparatus—equipment for heating, cooling, and collecting the liquor. Note the long lengths of coiled copper tubing for condensing the alcohol. The Duquettes' setup probably consisted of two or three pieces similar to those displayed in the photo below.

Even though his own experiences with Prohibition were far more benign, Duquette still finds himself in opposition to the law. "Prohibition just wasn't a good thing," he said thoughtfully. "The law created more problems than it solved."

Duquette still vividly remembers December 5, 1933, the day Prohibition was repealed. Hearing that it was legal to drink for the first time in thirteen years—and the first time in his adult life—he rounded up some friends and went into the village. At the Crystal Lake Hotel, which stood on its shores many years ago, the group ordered a round. Raising a beer that cost Duquette only a nickel, he said, "To a drink with friends, and to my father's morning glass, which he can finally have again without worrying about being arrested," and they all laughed.

CHAPTER 16

Ida Tabor
"Deliveries on Horseback"

Ida Tabor of Newport, Vermont, was no more than fourteen when she stumbled into the lucrative business of selling moonshine. "I liked the fun in it, and I liked the money, too," said the feisty ninety-one-year-old woman who prefers to be called Ida.

Living with her parents, Hermidas and Virginia Lebeau, in Evansville, a small town in Orleans County, Ida got into the moonshine business innocently enough. "I was hanging around the blacksmith's shop, where people used to gather, when a local man asked me if I'd run an errand for him." The errand turned out to be picking up a gallon of moonshine from a farmer who operated a still in his sugarhouse. It was a cold night, and when Ida hesitated, the man made an offer she couldn't turn down—the loan of his heavy wool hunting pants to keep her warm, and five dollars' pay—in an era when farm wages were often only ten dollars a week. Ida pulled on the warm trousers and mounted her horse. "Here's five dollars for the whiskey," her thirsty customer told her, "and there'll be five more for you when you get back."

Ida rode out through the dark, snowy night to the farm and handed over the money. The farmer gave her a gallon jug and a dollar in change, and Ida headed back into town. When she returned to the blacksmith's shop, her customer thanked her, took the jug, and paid her five dollars. Ida knew she had discovered easy money, and that trip was the first of many she made before Prohibition was repealed in 1933.

Ida's parents barely had enough money to keep their farm operating and their children fed. "Those were tough times, and there was no spending money or luxuries for us children," Ida said. With true entrepreneurial spirit, Ida decided she didn't have to wait for the occasional request to go buy a jug of moonshine; she started buying and re-selling booze herself.

Just down the road from Evansville was the larger town of Orleans, where Ida saw a business opportunity: The town had a number of sheds where people kept their horses and buggies while they did business. The sheds were also favorite meeting places for local men who sat, chatted, and drank. When alcohol was not available, some of the men drank vanilla extract, which had a high concentration of alcohol. "A bottle of the stuff was enough to give a person a buzz," Ida said.

Young Ida scoured each shed for the discarded bottles of all types, collecting them as she went. Once her rounds were completed, she returned home to clean the bottles. Ida bought moonshine from the farmer for four dollars a gallon and decanted it into

Reusing bottles, Tabor launched her lucrative bootlegging business. This one originally contained not vanilla, but "The Great Restorative E.S. Burnham's Beef, Wine & Iron Tonic." One of the principal ingredients of most tonics was alcohol. Prohibition, combined with the food purity acts of 1920s, led to the demise of many such patent medicines, including those made by Wells & Richardson in Burlington, Vermont.

sixteen of the eight-ounce vanilla bottles. She carefully packed the small bottles in a burlap bag, slung the bag across her horse's back, climbed into the saddle, and rode off to sell the liquor. Some of her best customers were loggers. "Having a horse instead of a car was good for business," Ida noted. "With a horse I could go deep into the woods to the logging sites, to places where no car could go." With only hand tools at their disposal—axes, saws, and peaveys—the loggers worked up quite a thirst cutting wood all day, and they looked forward to her visits.

Tabor had a good business going. She sold her little bottles for seventy-five cents apiece, netting her eight dollars' profit for every gallon she sold. Ida's business was so brisk that she recalls selling approximately five gallons' worth of the tiny bottles of booze per week. Suddenly, Ida was able to help the family, buying things her parents couldn't afford. Eventually she even saved enough for her first car, a Willys-Knight.

Ida occasionally passed lawmen as she plodded along on her horse. "They didn't ever bother me," she said with a smile. She greeted the unwitting officers, who apparently never suspected what sort of cargo she might be carrying, and allowed her to continue on her way. "I was young and I was a girl, so they didn't pay much attention to me."

Like any distributor, Ida needed a warehouse. She used her family's barn, burying her bottles in the haymow or the grain bins. Ida didn't like to keep much alcohol around, however, in case her home was visited by lawmen or federal revenuers.

One year, with Christmas nearing and the family unable to make ends meet, Ida hatched a plot with her uncle: They would brew a little moonshine of their own. "We rigged up a contraption to serve as a still," she said, "and made our mash using cracked corn, sugar, and yeast. The idea was working fine," Ida said, laughing, "until my uncle decided to sample it for himself. By the time he was done sampling, most of the booze and all of our profits had been drunk up. He drank the liquor before it got cold, so there was no extra money for Christmas.

"When I saw what he was up to, I got mad at him and said, 'No more!' and then in frustration tossed the mash across the room, making a great mess on the floor. That was a mistake," Ida recalled. "My family's chickens and ducks ate the mash and were soon staggering around. At first, I thought my uncle had done something that poisoned the birds, and I was going to kill him. Then we figured out that they were just drunk. That was the last time I ever did any moonshining with my uncle."

Reflecting on her youth, Ida, now a small, spirited great-grand-mother, said with a mischievous look that she was a wild girl who kept her parents on their toes. They didn't approve of their daughter's behavior or her activities, and tried to convince her to stop. "My parents told me that if I got caught and jailed, they'd bring me cheese and crackers, but I shouldn't expect them to bail me out." The threat didn't have the desired effect.

To this day, Ida professes her innocence about the episode that landed her in jail. When she was sixteen there was a big barn dance in St. Johnsbury, about thirty miles south of the family's home. She and her brother wanted to go, but their father wouldn't let them. An older, married friend named Walter convinced Tabor, her brother, and another friend, Ernest, to ride along with him to the dance, reassuring them that their parents would never find out about the trip. "We had a high-o time," Ida said.

Ida and her brother didn't drink, but the others did. While Walter was spending time with a girlfriend, Ida, her brother, and Ernest decided to go for a drive. Ida was behind the wheel and her brother was in the front passenger's seat, while a drunken Ernest was installed in the backseat. Eventually the trio drew the attention of two state troopers who decided to stop Ida and her companions.

"'Where you fellows going?' one officer asked me, and I replied, 'We're not going anywhere.'"

"He then asked, 'Do you have any alcohol in your vehicle?' My brother and I replied that we didn't drink.

"Observing Ernest acting strangely in the backseat, the officer asked Ernest to let him smell his breath to see if he'd been drink-

It's "chicken-hooch" in this town, One drink and you lay!

Whether or not Ernest was drinking "chicken-hooch," he was probably drinking something stronger than its pre-Prohibition counterpart. During Prohibition the proof of most drinks increased dramatically, on average, by 150%.

ing. That's when the trouble began. Ernest, usually a quiet, demure man, offered the lawman a slurred suggestion of his own: 'Why don't you smell my ass instead?'

The now-irked officer then turned back to Ida and asked to see her driver's license. She said she didn't have one and tried to convince the officer that Ernest was teaching her to drive that very night.

"'Some teacher,' the officer scoffed. 'Why, he's so drunk he doesn't even know his own name!'" Ida chuckled at the memory.

"The troopers weren't having any of this. They made the three of us leave our car beside the road, get in with them, and then they took us right to jail," Ida said.

The two men were put in the crowded jail, but the Caledonia County sheriff's wife took pity on the girl. "She didn't want me in jail with all those drunks, so I stayed with the sheriff and his family in their home, which was connected to the jail." In the meantime, the sheriff got a message to Tabor's parents that she and her brother and their friend were in jail, and needed somebody to bail them out.

When the sheriff's wife asked Ida if she was scared about having been arrested, Ida replied that she was more scared of her father. In the morning, Ida's father and her friend's father arrived and begrudgingly paid their bail: thirteen dollars apiece. "Our fathers were mad as hell, and boy, weren't they kicking our butts and knocking us around," she said. "Things got rough enough that it was only the sheriff's threats to arrest them that made them stop. In fact, they probably wouldn't have bailed us out so quickly if it weren't for the fact that there was hay to get in, and they needed our help," Ida said.

Later, Ida began traveling the twenty-five miles north to Canada to dance and have a good time. One of her favorite destinations was Spooner's Line House, which straddled the Canadian border in Derby, Vermont. "It was a tough place," said Ida. "There were no rules. There was a lot of drinking and a lot of fighting, but nobody ever bothered me. I took care of myself very good," she says with a self-assured smile. "On some trips I brought bottles of alcohol back with me to sell. That wasn't so easy." Buying the alcohol in Canada was no problem, but getting it back into Vermont—past the lawmen who watched the border crossings and patrolled many of the area's back roads—was a different story.

Ida brought only a few bottles across at a time, and she often did so in the company of an older female friend who wasn't afraid of being caught. "My friend did like her liquor," Tabor said. Making their way back from Canada into the state, the woman hid the bottles where few Customs officers dared venture—under her dress. Ida remembers one time during the holidays when a Customs officer questioned her and her friend at the border. The older woman was drunk and had a dress full of booze at the time. "My friend said, 'Officer, would you like me to get out and wish you a good New Year's with kisses and hugs?' The agent quickly declined the offer, and we were on our way back into Vermont.

The U.S. Customs and Immigration facility in Derby Line, Vermont, where Tabor and her traveling companion may well have re-entered the country.

"Purchasing alcohol from a reliable source was important," said Ida. "Some people sold booze made with bad ingredients such as rubbing alcohol, which could be deadly," said Tabor. "Others diluted their booze with water." Death from bad alcohol was a frequent occurrence during Prohibition. The August 9, 1932 issue of the *Palladium and News*, a now-defunct Orleans County newspaper, reported a gruesome story about the tragic effects of bad alcohol on a family in South Troy, Vermont. Crazed from the effects of poisoned moonshine, a man killed his wife and four-year-old-son with shotgun blasts to their heads, then took his own life with a .22 revolver. Unfortunately, these incidents were all too common.

Ida said with a sense of pride that in the illegal booze trade, she developed a reputation as an honest person who dealt only in good booze made with quality ingredients. Looking back on her long life, Tabor said, "I have no regrets about my activities during Prohibition, because it was a bad law." After a brief pause, she smiled and continued. "It did get me into my next line of work, though." For many years after the repeal in 1933, Tabor tended bar in Newport, Vermont, at The Snake Pit, a rowdy establishment once located in the basement of the long-gone Newport Hotel.

CHAPTER 17

John Pfeifer:
"The Border Today"

The more things change, the more they stay the same—an apt description of the Vermont–Quebec border. Smuggling continues to be a major activity along the border, and alcohol still motivates many crossings. Nowadays, the smuggled alcohol is heading north to Canada, where legal alcohol is much more expensive than in the U.S. As before, many Vermonters travel north to Quebec to drink, these days to take advantage of the province's drinking age of eighteen, compared to Vermont's strictly enforced twenty-one.

Alcohol-related deaths remain an all-too-common occurrence in the region. During Prohibition, lawmen were shot and killed by ruthless smugglers, and smugglers were shot and killed by over-zealous lawmen. Most alcohol-related deaths today are the result of automobile fatalities that occur as younger Vermonters return home from a night of drinking in Quebec.

The people and territory remain knit together much as they were seventy years ago. Hundreds of miles of road, many still unpaved, interlace the region. In some towns streets are literally divided by the international border, with neighbors living in different countries. An ice arena in Stanstead, Quebec, serves as the home ice for the Newport, Vermont, North Country Union High School hockey team. The historic Haskell Opera House straddles the border, with the stage in Quebec and the audience in Vermont.

While ties between communities on both sides of the border continue to flourish, the September 11, 2001, terrorist attacks on

New York and Washington have altered the relationship, especially at the once-lenient border crossings. Before the attacks, "locals" on both sides could typically cross the border with a wave of the hand to officers staffing the port of entry. Now everyone is scrutinized, and even familiar faces may find themselves subject to spot checks. On the American side, National Guardsmen flank their Customs and Immigration colleagues, giving the once-friendly border the feel of a military checkpoint.

Historically, residents have been proud of the border's openness. Few, however, have complained about the added security. Nonetheless, many yearn for a return to the atmosphere of earlier days, before the terrorist attacks, when people scarcely felt the border's presence. Agents are on the alert not only for the familiar contraband of illegal booze, drugs, and aliens, but also for new threats, including bombs and bomb-making materials. Only a few

Founded in 1924, the United States Border Patrol was an outgrowth of the Mounted Inspectors, who used horses to patrol their territories. In the early days, the government provided agents with only a badge and a service revolver; agents had to supply their own horse and saddle. The pay? The government supplied hay and oats for the horse, and a $1680 salary for the agent.

The Patrol has continually modernized and expanded, first adding cars, and subsequently boats, airplanes, and helicopters. The horses remain, however, as they provide mobility unmatched by any other technology.

years ago, some would-be terrorists crossed the border into Richford, Vermont. They carried with them a bomb destined for some undisclosed target; fortunately, they were apprehended by vigilant officers who foiled their plans.

The recently stepped-up border security appears to have altered the flow of illegal substances as well. John Pfeifer, Patrol Agent in Charge of the Border Patrol Station in Newport, Vermont, said that while high-grade marijuana continues to be moved from Canada into the U.S., the flow of alcohol to Canada has nearly dried up. Pfeifer estimates that the trafficking of alcohol has dropped by 90 percent since 9/11.

Pfeifer, a commonsense, straight-talking lawman, is a sixteen-year veteran of the patrol. He has worked on both America's southern and northern borders, and has, by his own account, seen his share of action, even suffering a gunshot wound on one occasion. Despite having been subjected to such personal violence, Pfeifer remains very positive about his work and respectful of the rights of all parties—even those on the wrong side of the law.

Pfeifer emphasized that the while his agency is responsible for patrolling the border, it receives vital outside assistance. "We work hand-in-hand with many other agencies to accomplish our mission. We routinely work with the U.S. Customs Service, the Vermont State Police, and a number of county-level and local law enforcement agencies. We also coordinate our efforts with the Royal Canadian Mounted Police."

Back during Prohibition federal officers occasionally resorted to gunfire to stop fleeing automobiles—shooting at their tires and gas tanks, and sometimes accidentally killing the vehicle's occupants. Pfeifer said agents generally no longer use firepower to stop an escaping car. Instead, they employ modern technologies, such as radios and helicopters, to help them capture suspects.

"We're not going to use deadly force to stop someone smuggling alcohol into or out of the United States," he said. "In fact, it isn't the job of the Border Patrol to stop alcohol smugglers heading north into Canada," Pfeifer said.

"The Border Patrol was formed in 1924 to detect and prevent the illegal entry of aliens; we also arrest aliens who overstay their legal entry or who enter under false pretenses. False pretenses, explains Pfeifer, arise when people entering the country give agents false answers when asked to reveal the nature of their visit to the U.S. "When someone tells us that they're entering Vermont to visit for pleasure, but then they go to New Hampshire and buy large quantities of alcohol to bring back into Canada, they have broken U.S. Immigration Laws."

"People smuggle alcohol because there is easy money to be made," said Pfeifer. "Currently there is a great financial incentive to smuggle alcohol, which costs two to three times more in Canada than in the States." New Hampshire is a favorite destination for smugglers because there is also no tax on alcohol. Pfeifer noted that many of the alcohol smugglers are running alcohol for bar owners, some of whom are members of notorious, outlaw biker gangs operating in Quebec's Eastern Townships.

While the motives for smuggling have changed little, technology has changed the way that law enforcement agencies operate. While Prohibition lawmen sometimes had to patrol in makeshift confiscated cars, agents today have sophisticated vehicles with two-way radios. Since the September 11 attacks, the Border Patrol has even taken to the air in a helicopter, giving them a fast-moving, bird's-eye view of the region.

During the days of Prohibition, officers relied mainly on a combination of good luck and the cooperation of informants who lived along the smuggling roots to alert them to illegal entries. Some ports of entry weren't even located on the border, but were nearby in town. Reporting in was a matter of honesty, and smugglers

John C. Pfeifer, Patrol Agent In Charge, U.S. Border Patrol, stands outside the Newport, Vermont station, 2002.

exploited this fact. In addition, officers were so scarce and roads so plentiful that the odds of a smuggler falling into the hands of lawmen were slim.

While Border Patrol officers still rely on the eyes of those living along the border, their task has been made much easier and more effective by detection devices strategically deployed along the border. Video cameras and motion detectors monitor unguarded roads and mountainous, forested areas of the border, where humans seldom tread. They immediately report any potentially illegal entry. "A higher percentage of smugglers are now nabbed soon after entering the country," Pfeifer said. "Yet, there is no way of knowing how many other smugglers and illegal aliens slip through our grasp."

Some modern-day alcohol smugglers operate in much the same fashion as their Prohibition counterparts. For instance, they may drive old vehicles they can afford to lose if confiscated. Some attempt to conceal the bottles, using out-of-the-way locations such as the engine compartment, the radiator, or the underside of the

2001: an SUV full of liquor. Smugglers are still very much interested in taking alcohol over the border. The agents of the Swanton Sector, which is responsible for 261 miles of border located in Vermont, New Hampshire, and New York, caught this smuggler bringing liquor back to Canada. The modern-day bootlegger was stopped and the goods were seized, netting 86 cases of liquor worth an estimated $5,300 US.

car. Smugglers who are handling hundreds of bottles of booze at a time usually have no inclination to give up any potential cargo space. More importantly, they have no plans to stop at the border on their trip north.

"Weighted down with hundreds of bottles of booze," Pfeifer said, "the smuggling cars are easy to pick out as they travel north. They are the cars with their rear ends sagging, often almost to the ground." Sometimes agents stop them immediately; other times they'll keep an eye on the vehicle while radioing Canadian authorities that a smuggler is about to jump the border. Once they cross the border, often using an unguarded road or a route through a farmer's field, the smugglers are in real trouble. Not only are Canadian authorities likely to charge them with smuggling alcohol into Quebec, but they will also add the charge of entering Canada illegally.

The unending cat-and-mouse game of smuggling ensures that border agents constantly encounter novel approaches to getting booze over the border. Pfeifer described the strategy of one group of Canadians that went to great lengths.

The smugglers traveled to New Hampshire and bought hundreds of bottles of liquor; then they drove to a trailer in West Derby, Vermont, located right on the border. They dumped the liquor into five-gallon water jugs and saved the empty bottles. From the trailer they had run a garden hose underground across the border to a second trailer on the Quebec side. They poured

While some smugglers may use subtle and ingenious mechanisms to convey alcohol over the border, other smugglers don't seem to feel the need for such cleverness and devise remarkably inept schemes, such as loading the back of an open pick-up truck with 372 bottles of liquor and then hoping no one will notice.

the liquor into a tub and used a sump pump to send it across the border to the other trailer, where it was rebottled.

The incessant humming of the pump aroused the curiosity of nearby residents, whose concerns eventually led to an investigation by various law agencies. The inquiries culminated in the arrest of the smugglers and the end of their operation.

"That was the most unique operation I've ever seen," Pfeifer said.

At least for now.

EPILOGUE

The attitudes of Prohibition-era Vermonters toward alcohol were complex and divergent. After all, Vermonters themselves had voted to keep the state "dry" for all but one year between 1847 and 1903. It would be more truthful, though, to say that the state was "damp," as the law was loosely enforced and often disregarded.

The varied responses of residents to the state's sanctions against alcohol reveals a well-known propensity for independent thinking in the citizenry. Even today, nothing raises the hackles of Vermonters more than do government mandates, especially those emanating from Washington. Back in 1920, when the federal government instituted Prohibition, the stage was set for conflict.

From 1920 to 1933, rumrunners on the lake, bootleggers on Vermont's back roads, and moonshiners in the hills kept up an active and defiant trade in alcohol. Many were lured by easy money, and most were bolstered by an ornery disregard for Prohibition and government interference. The Law had to respond, and did—joining smugglers and revenuers in battle. With the repeal of Prohibition in 1933, the struggle ended, but the character of the original players lives on today in the Kingdom.

SOURCES

There is a large literature focused on national Prohibition. Most of the following sources have a Vermont focus:

Clifford, Deborah P. "The Women's War Against Rum" in *Vermont History* (Montpelier: Vermont Historical Society, volume 52, summer 1984), 141-160.

Holmes, Beatrice, S., *History of Canaan Vermont*. Colebrook, New Hampshire: M/S Printing & Advertising, 1976 + 1998.

Kerr, K. Austin, Temperance and Prohibition website. Ohio State University Department of History: *http://prohibition.history.ohiostate.edu.*

McCutcheon, Marc. *The Writer's Guide to Everyday Life from Prohibition through World War II*. Cincinnati, Ohio: Writer's Digest Books, 1995.

"Millennium Project." Burlington, Vermont: Vermont Business Magazine, 1999.

Pegram, Thomas, R., *Battling Demon Rum: The Struggle for a Dry America, 1800 – 1933*. Chicago, Illinois: Ivan R. Dee, 1998.

Prohibition: Thirteen Years That Changed America. Narrated by Ed Asner. BBC Television/A&E/ARTE.

Rose, Kenneth D. *American Women and the Repeal of Prohibition*. New York, New York: New York University Press, 1996.

Soule, Bradley A., MD. "The United States Customs Boat Patrol on Lake Champlain During Prohibition Era" in *Vermont History* (Montpelier: Vermont Historical Society, volume 48, summer 1980), 133-143.

Thornton, Mark. "Alcohol Prohibition was a Failure" in *Policy Analysis* (Washington DC: Cato Institute, number 157, July 17, 1991), 1-15.

United States Border Patrol, Swanton and Derby stations

United States Department of Customs, Highgate, Vermont

Vermont Historical Society, Barre, Vermont

Vermont State Archives, Montpelier, Vermont